Top 25 locator map
(continues on inside
back cover)

C000216634

TwinPack
Gran Canaria

GABRIELLE MACPHEDRAN

Gabrielle MacPhedran, journalist and broadcaster, is the author of several guidebooks, including *AA Essential Berlin*, *AA Essential Canary Islands* and *AA Explorer Spain*. She is a regular contributor to the Daily and Sunday Telegraph, The Times, Country Magazine and other periodicals. She lives in Sussex with her travel-writer husband, Adam Hopkins.

If you have any comments or suggestions for this guide you can contact the editor at *Twinpacks@theAA.com*

AA Publishing
Find out more about AA Publishing and the wide range of travel publications and services the AA provides by visiting our website at *www.theAA.com/bookshop*

Contents

About this book

KEY TO SYMBOLS

✚ Grid reference to the Top 25 locator map

✉ Address

☎ Telephone number

🕐 Opening/closing times

🍴 Restaurant or café on premises or near by

🚇 Nearest underground (tube) station

🚉 Nearest railway station

🚌 Nearest bus route

⛴ Nearest riverboat or ferry stop

♿ Facilities for visitors with disabilities

✋ Admission charge

↔ Other nearby places of interest

❓ Tours, lectures or special events

➤ Indicates the page where you will find a fuller description

ℹ Tourist information

TwinPack Gran Canaria is divided into six sections. It includes:

- The author's view of the island and its people
- Suggested walks and excursions
- The Top 25 sights to visit – as selected by the author
- The best of the rest – aspects of the island that make it special
- Detailed listings of restaurants, hotels, shops and nightlife
- Practical information

In addition, easy-to-read side panels provide fascinating extra facts and snippets, highlights of places to visit and invaluable practical advice.

CROSS-REFERENCES

To help you make the most of your visit, cross-references, indicated by ➤, show you where to find additional information about a place or subject.

MAPS

The fold-out map in the wallet at the back of the book is a large-scale island map of Gran Canaria.

The Top 25 locator maps found on the inside front and back covers of the book itself are for quick reference. They show the Top 25 Sights, described on pages 24–48, which are clearly plotted by number (**1**–**25**, not page number) in alphabetical order.

PRICES

Where appropriate, an indication of the cost of an establishment is given by € signs: €€€ denotes higher prices, €€ denotes average prices, while € denotes lower charges.

GRAN CANARIA life

A Personal View

This Spanish island in the deeps of the Atlantic Ocean, closer to Africa than to Europe, and small enough to drive round in a day, attracts more than two and a half million visitors every year. The reason for its popularity? Year round sunshine, never too hot or too cold (average max: 24°C, min: 19°C, summer or winter).

Most people head for the southern resorts like San Agustín, Playa del Inglés and Maspalomas, now merged into a continuous tourist strip to

become one of the largest beach resorts in the whole of Spain. The first sight of this cityscape of high-rise hotels and apartments, fast food joints and flashing neon is often daunting. Such concentrated mass tourism does not suit everyone, but within a distance of six or seven kilometres, the receptive visitor will soon distinguish between the cheerful ebullience of Playa del Inglés, the more reserved atmosphere of San Agustín and the glamour and glitz of some Maspalomas enclaves.

Above: fishing boats in Puerto de Mogán
Right: cool benches in Firgas

Deep-sea fishermen head for Puerto Rico, windsurfers prefer Pozo Izquierdo, golfers can choose between Maspalomas in the south or highly picturesque Bandama in the interior. Those who prefer a historic centre, an urban environment and cooler weather opt to stay in Las Palmas, the capital of the island which, incidentally, boasts one of its best beaches.

As with all the Canary Islands, the landscape of Gran Canaria was created by a series of volcanic eruptions. It is strange, spectacular and diverse. The south of the island is arid, desert-like and, since the 1960s, devoted almost entirely to tourism. To the west, the island rises to cliffs of jagged black rock, pounded by powerful seas. Among the green northern hills clouds can blot out the sun for hours at a time, and there is occasional snowfall on the highest volcanic peaks of its centre. This climatic diversity produces, in its turn, a vast range of flora. Pine, heather, and broom, mango and papaya, lavender and asphodel, palm and enormous candle-stick euphorbia can all be seen within a half hour's drive into the interior.

Apart from the main road that traces the circumference of the island, most island roads – uniformly well maintained – follow the declivity of the gorges or *barrancos* that run from the centre down to the sea. Most visitors hire a car for a day or two to explore the island. Buses, known as *guaguas*, are cheap and efficiently run, connecting most of the towns and villages. As for walkers, in a splendid landscape crisscrossed by a multiplicity of pack-animal tracks and old ways between villages, they naturally count themselves blessed on Gran Canaria.

COUNTRY WAYS

Most of the island's population now lives by tourism and many young people have left behind the hard agricultural life of their parents in their villages to find work in the tourist resorts. However, family ties and rural roots remain strong. Young Canarios return home to celebrate village fiestas and maintain the island traditions of folk dance and song. The Canarian sport of wrestling or *lucha canaria* is popular and there are classes to teach and maintain the old pre-hispanic Guanche sport of fighting with poles or garrote.

Gran Canaria in Figures

GEOGRAPHY

- Gran Canaria is in the Atlantic Ocean 210km from the African coastline and 1,250km from Cádiz in mainland Spain.
- Its highest point is Pozo de las Nieves (1,949m).
- The average temperature in summer is 24°C; in winter it's 19°C.
- The wettest part is the north of the island with an average annual rainfall of 500mm.
- The range of altitudes ensures the presence of plants from almost every climatic zone.
- The largest mammal to live wild on the island is the rabbit.
- With an area of 1,532sq km, Gran Canaria is third largest of the seven major islands of the Canarian archipelago. The largest islands are Tenerife and Fuerteventura. Gran Canaria has the greatest population.
- It is a circular, volcanic island which last erupted seriously about 3,000 years ago. The land comes steeply down from the high central peaks, with vast *barrancos* – dry water courses or ravines – running to the coast like the spokes of a bicycle wheel.

PEOPLE

- The population of the island is 700,000, of which 400,000 live in the city of Las Palmas. In 1991 the population of the Canary Islands was 1.6 million.
- The capital city is Las Palmas, which is also capital of the province bearing the same name. This consists of Gran Canaria and the other eastern islands, Fuerteventura and Lanzarote.
- The western islands, including Tenerife, La Palma, Gomera and El Hierro, form the province of Tenerife. Together, since 1983, the two provinces have made up the Autonomous Region of the Canary Islands.

LANGUAGE

- Spanish is the official language, though English is widely spoken in the main tourist areas.

TOURISM

- Around 2,800,000 tourists visit Gran Canaria every year.

People of Gran Canaria

Jean de Béthencourt
Charged by Henry III of Castile with conquering the Canary Islands, this Norman soldier (1359–1426) set out in 1402 with his lieutenant Gadifer de la Salle and took the island of Lanzarote, for which he was awarded the title 'King of the Canary Islands'. He next conquered Fuerteventura. However, the aboriginal people of Gran Canaria resisted him successfully, and he returned to France.

Christopher Columbus
Born in Genoa, in modern-day Italy, Christopher Columbus (1451–1506) persuaded the Catholic monarchs, Ferdinand and Isabella of Spain, to sponsor his expedition to find a western route to India. Instead of the Orient he found the New World. On his first, second and fourth voyages across the Atlantic, Columbus put in at Gran Canaria. The house where he stayed and the church in which he prayed lie in the Vegueta district of Las Palmas (► 35).

Benito Pérez Galdós
Pérez Galdós (1843–1920), the 'Charles Dickens of Spain', was the youngest child in a family of 10, born to an army officer and his wife in Calle Cano 6 in the Triana district of Las Palmas, now a museum. He studied as a lawyer in Madrid before becoming a novelist and playwright. The island is extremely proud of Pérez Galdós, although he lived his adult life on the Spanish mainland. His best known work is Episodios Nacionales, a historical novel in 46 volumes.

Néstor Martín Fernández de la Torre
Artist Néstor (1887–1938) studied at the Academy of Fine Art in Madrid but always kept his roots alive in the city of his birth, Las Palmas. Many of his canvases – such as Poema del Atlántico – depict aspects of the island in a romantic, free-flowing manner. See his work at the Museo Néstor (► 52) in the Pueblo Canario. He painted the murals in the Teatro Galdós, shocking bourgeois sensibilities and, less controversially, designed the Tejeda *parador*.

NAME-DROPPING

Other names the visitor may encounter which are famous on the island but not widely known elsewhere include: Nicolas Estévanez y Murphy, poet; Francisco Guerra Navarro (Pancho Guerra), novelist; León y Castillo, engineer; José Luján Pérez, sculptor and religious painter; Tomás Morales Castellano, poet; Alonso Quesada, poet; José Viera y Clavijo, historian and natural historian.

A Chronology

3000 BC–1500 AD | The island is inhabited by Cro-Magnon and Mediterranean-type stone age people, who wear skins, keep livestock and grow cereals. They have no written language.

1st century AD | First mention of the name 'Canaria', by the historian Pliny the Elder. He calls the archipelago 'The Fortunate Isles'.

13th century AD | Arrival of slaving expeditions from the rest of Europe.

1340–42 | Portuguese and Spanish send expeditions from Mallorca.

1405 | The Norman Jean de Béthencourt (▶ 9) fails in his attempt to conquer Gran Canaria for the Spanish throne.

1478 | Juan Rejón founds the city of Real de las Palmas and begins subduing the island. The aboriginal people are led by two kings: Tenesor Semidan, who rules the west of the island from his base at Gáldar, and Doramas, chief of the east, who rules from Telde. Rejón wins the first major battle.

1480 | Under the Treaty of Alcáçovas, Portugal renounces her claims to the Canary Islands.

1481 | The Guanche king Doramas is killed at Montana de Arucas.

1482 | The Guanche king Tenesor Semidan is captured, taken to Spain and baptised as 'Fernando Guanarteme'. He then joins the Spanish cause.

1483 | Siege of Ansite. Most Canarios surrender. Others throw themselves off cliffs. The end of aboriginal resistance.

1492 | Christopher Columbus anchors in Las Palmas for repairs to his ships on his first expedition to the New World. He returns there on his second and fourth voyages.

1496–c1525	Intensive colonisation by Spaniards, Portuguese and Italians. Portuguese bring knowledge of sugar cane industry from Madeira.
Early 16th century	Growing prosperity for Gran Canaria from trade with the New World and cultivation of sugar cane.
18th and 19th centuries	After collapse of the sugar trade, following competition from the New World, main exports are wine and cochineal (the insects which produce the dye are bred and fed on prickly pear).
1820	Las Palmas becomes the capital of Gran Canaria.
1852	The Canaries are declared a free trade zone in an effort to boost the islands' economy.
Early 20th century	Intensive cultivation of bananas and tomatoes.
1927	Canary Islands are divided into two provinces; poverty results in emigration to Latin America.
1936	General Franco visits Gran Canaria and launches the military coup which begins the Spanish Civil War (1936–39).
1950s	Canarians demand home rule.
1960s	Plans to develop the south for tourism.
1970s	Mass tourism arrives: tomato fields give way to hotels.
1975	Death of Franco.
1978	Spain becomes a constitutional monarchy under King Juan Carlos I.
1983	Spanish devolution leads to greater autonomy for the islands.
1989	Canary Islands become full members of the European Community (as part of Spain).
2002	Canary Islands introduce the euro.

Best of Gran Canaria

Puerto de Mogán, the most westerly resort on the island

If you only have a short time to visit Gran Canaria and are looking for the best way to experience the essence of the island, here are some suggestions for activities and places that shouldn't be missed.

- Watch the sunset over the sea from the lighthouse at Maspalomas, as fishermen cast their lines from the rocks and the shadows deepen among the dunes.
- Take a boat trip from Arguineguín or Puerto Rico to Puerto de Mogán (➤ 42), last resort village on the west coast, for a view of the island from the sea.
- Walk in the Tamadaba pine forest (➤ 46), with soft pine needles underfoot and undergrowth of cistus and thyme. Look down to the harbour at Puerto de las Nieves, far below, and across the sea to Mount Teide on Tenerife.
- Linger in the sun at a terrace café in the Parque Santa Catalina (➤ 55) in Las Palmas. Watch the locals play chess and dominoes at outdoor tables.
- Visit the ancient religious site of the island's aboriginal people at Cuatro Puertas (➤ 52). Look from the top of the windswept hill to imagine a time before the Spaniards arrived.
- Have a coffee in the lounge of the Hotel Santa Catalina (➤ 81) in Las Palmas. All celebrity visitors to the island stay here, including King Juan Carlos.
- See a Canarian wrestling match, or *lucha canaria*, a team sport descended from pre-Spanish, Guanche times which sends the restrained Canarios wild with excitement.
- Drive eastwards from Pasito Blanco on the old coast road at night for a sudden view, as you crest the hill, of the lights of Maspalomas and Playa del Inglés, like a shimmering blanket of stars.
- Catch a performance of Canarian folk singing and dancing back in Las Palmas at the Pueblo Canario (➤ 52) on Sunday morning at 11:30.

GRAN CANARIA
how to organise your time

13

A Walk Around Historic Las Palmas

This walk starts at Calle Mayor de Triana, the shopping street that leads down to Vegueta, the old city. After visiting Vegueta, it returns to historic Plaza de Cairasco.

Walk south from the hermitage of San Telmo on pedestrianised Calle Mayor de Triana. Note the Art Nouveau buildings, starting at No 98.

Finally, angle left at the statue of Juan Negrín. At the major highway, go one block left to Teatro Pérez Galdós. Return and cross over to the market (Mercado de Las Palmas), on the left. Continue on along Calle Mendizábal, then right up handsome Calle de los Balcones.

Here the local and national artistic heritage is on display at CAAM (Centro Atlántico de Arte Moderno, ▶ 52).

In Plaza del Pilar turn right, following the east side of the Colón house. At the next small square the church of San Antonio Abad is to the right, and a few steps further down to the right is the Montesdeoca restaurant. Return and follow the north side of Colón house (entrance on left). Continue straight ahead into Plaza de Santa Ana and turn left, passing the cathedral façade.

The cathedral museum (▶ 29) is 25m left at the next turning, in Espiritu Santo.

Retrace your steps 25m to the end of Espiritu Santo. Turn left into Calle Reloj and walk to Calle Dr Chil. Turn right. The Museo Canario (▶ 38) is on the left.

Passing the Museo, continue 60m up Calle Dr Chil, then angle sharply back into Plaza de Santa Ana. From the cathedral front, exit left down Calle Obispo Codina. Cross the highway and go straight on into Plaza de Cairasco.

Here you can enjoy a drink outside the Hotel Madrid, where Franco spent the night on the eve of the insurrection of the generals in 1936.

INFORMATION

Distance 2km
Time 1½ hours strolling, four hours with visits to attractions
Start point Parque de San Telmo
End point Plaza de Cairasco
🏨 Hotel Madrid (€)
✉ Plaza de Cairasco 2
☎ 928 36 06 64
❓ Alternatively many cafés and bars in market area

Ornamental architecture in Las Palmas

A Drive Around the South

This drive takes you from the coast to the central highlands, through one *barranco*, and back down another.

Take the coast road to Arguineguín. At the roundabout behind the cement factory turn right, under the motorway, for Cercado de Espina. Continue north into the *barranco*. At Cercado de Espina (12km) take the slip road right through the village. Soon, a steep, zig-zag climb begins, with wonderful views. At El Baranquillo Andrés (6km) a left turn is signed Mogán and Tejeda.

Another option is to continue onwards into Soria village, with its reservoir and restaurants, and then carry on to join the GC605 to Tejeda.

On the main route, turn left at Baranquillo Andrés. An asphalt road – probably best to use a 4WD vehicle – ascends through Z-bends to meet the main (dirt) road ascending from Mogán. Turn right here for Tejeda. The road soon runs close to a reservoir – Embalse de la Cueva de las Niñas – where there are agreeable picnic spots.

Continue 14km northeast through mountainous terrain for Ayacata. Turn right towards San Bartolomé de Tirajana; after 200m turn left (signed Los Pechos), climbing to pass Roque Nublo car park. Continue through pinewoods, finally taking a right turn for Los Pechos, arriving at Pico de las Nieves.

Again this part of the route offers fine views, as the ravine walls begin to narrow, of the great Roque Bermejo across the valley to the east.

Return to Ayacata and turn left to San Bartolomé. Follow signs for Fataga. A hairpin descent takes you into the much-admired Barranco de Fataga, passing Fataga village and Arteara. After a stiff climb out of the *barranco* the road passes Mundo Aborigen (► 37) and continues to Playa del Inglés.

INFORMATION

Distance Approximately 115km

Time About 5 hours driving

Start/end point Playa del Inglés

🍴 Casa Bar Melo (€)

✉ Cruce de Ayacata

☎ No phone

❓ Restaurants in Soria village (€–€€)

Driving up through the interior's twisting roads

Finding Peace & Quiet

Astonishingly, for an island as populous and popular as Gran Canaria, peace and quiet are easy to find. Even in the main tourist resorts, hotel gardens are often planted like miniature tropical forests.

INLAND RESERVOIRS

The reservoirs of Chira, Soria and Cueva de las Niñas, in the west central part of the island, offer areas to relax beside the water but away from the coast. In some places you can swim off a small beach or dive off rocks. It is possible to hike between all three reservoirs.

THE WEST COAST

The major road through the southern resorts leaves the coast abruptly at Puerto de Mogán (► 42) and shoots up the *barranco* into the mountains. Any beach from Playa de Mogán to Puerto de la Aldea at the island's northwestern tip is likely to offer solitude.

The beaches of Veneguera (sand), Tasarte (pebble) and Asno (rock and black sand) are all accessible on foot. It is possible to walk to Güigüí, the star of all remote beaches, but only for the hardy and sure-footed. Make a deal with a fishing boat from Puerto de la Aldea, Mogán or Puerto Rico to drop you there and pick you up. In the summer, there are regular boat trips to Güigüí from Puerto Rico.

NATIVE PLANTS

Gran Canaria is a botanist's delight, with a wide variety of vegetation. Common endemic species include *pinus canariensis*, or the Canary pine, which has the useful talent of regeneration after fire: new growth emerges from seemingly life-

The dragon tree has become a Canarian symbol

less, charred bark. The hard wood of this tree, called *tea*, is used for ceilings and balconies. The rock rose (*cistus symphytifolius*) and asphodel (*asphodelus microcarpus*) grow in pine forests.

The extraordinary-looking dragon tree (*dracaena draco*), closely related to the yucca plant, has become the botanical symbol of the Canary Islands. With branches

like the legs of a stumpy grey elephant, ending in a spiky green crown, this primitive form of plant life is extremely long-lived. Early Guanches dried the red resin of dragon trees, which they used as medicine and as a dye, and islanders still use it as a cure for toothache.

The Canarian palm (*phoenix canariensis*), found all over the island, is similar to the North African date palm but shorter, with larger, lusher leaves and a more perfect crown. The leaves are used for basket work and the trunk for making beehives.

Other frequently appearing plants include broom (*retama*), with distinctive yellow flowers in spring and summer; taginaste, which produces white or blue flowers in spring; verode, with pink or yellow flowers, and tabaiba, a species of euphorbia, whose sap is used – with care – in popular medicine (it can cause temporary blindness). The *cardón* or candelabra cactus is a many-branched native euphorbia, technically *euphorbia canariensis*. The sap is mixed with oil and used as a medicine.

Geraniums tumble over garden walls

WALKS

Several hiking groups offer accompanied walks in the more remote parts of the island. These are usually run by foreign residents and are often over-subscribed. If you walk alone, make sure someone knows where you are going and can raise the alarm if necessary.

21

What's On

JANUARY	Festival of the Three Kings, 6 January: gifts for the children.
FEBRUARY	Almond Blossom Festival, Tejeda and Valsequillo: song and dance, picnics, almond sweets and cakes. Carnival: street bands, parties and parades.
MARCH	Arguineguín celebrates the feast day of Santa Agueda.
MARCH/APRIL	*Semanta Santa* is celebrated during Holy Week throughout the island. Processions with sacred icons and religious sculptures take place.
LATE MAY/JUNE	Feast of Corpus Cristi (sometimes in May): the streets are decorated with flowers and sand. Anniversary of the foundation of Las Palmas.
JULY	*Fiestas del Carmen*,16 July: celebrated by all fishing villages. Feast day of Santiago, 25 July: Gáldar and San Bartolomé. Gáldar has Canarian wrestling, *romerias* (picnics) and traditional dancing.
AUGUST	*Bajada de la Rama* in Agaete, 4 August: probably the most popular festival on the island. From an ancient aboriginal rite of praying for rain, where local people climbed high into the pine forests and brought down branches to thrash the sea. Modern Canarios enjoy the opportunity to get wet and have a party.
SEPTEMBER	Feast of La Virgen del Pino (Our Lady of the Pine, the patron saint of the whole island) in Teror, , 8 September: pilgrims come from all over the island. Cartfuls of produce are placed before the image of the Virgin in the square and then dispensed to the poor. *Fiesta del Charco* in San Nicolás de Tolentino, 10 September.
OCTOBER	*Fiestas de Nuestra Señora del Rosario* (Our Lady of the Rosary), celebrated in Agüimes, 5 October: Canarian stick-fighting and wrestling. *La Naval*, 6 October in Las Palmas, commemorates the successful repulsion of the English privateer Francis Drake in 1595. *Fiesta de la Manza* on the first Sunday in October celebrates the apple festival in Valleseco, nr. Teror.
NOVEMBER	Festival of San Martín de Porres, Arinaga.
DECEMBER	*Fiesta de los Labradores*, Santa Lucía, 20 December: people celebrate by dressing in peasant costumes and carrying farming tools.

GRAN CANARIA's
top 25 sights

The sights are shown on the maps on the inside front cover and inside back cover, numbered **1**–**25** alphabetically.

Andén Verde

Andén Verde, or 'Green Platform', is the name given to a magnificent stretch of corniche road on the island's north-west coast.

Winding northeast along the cliff-face, the road offers thrilling glimpses downwards, by way of plummeting rock, to a vertiginously distant sea. Though the extent of the Andén Verde is a little vague, this most exciting part of the west coast effectively begins a short way north of San Nicolás de Tolentino.

Running just inland for 6km or so from San Nicolás, the road suddenly veers towards a gap in a hill-crest above the sea. There is a small car park here, the Mirador del Balcón, or Balcony Viewpoint. Though views from the car park are very fine, it is worth descending the few steps to a lower platform. From here the rocks below and the cliff foot to the southwest, may be seen

The spectacular road on the Andén Verde

clearly. The cliff is surmounted by a dramatic series of hills, each of them terminating suddenly in a triangle of dark cliff. Each successive triangle is a little lower than the one before, their diminishing height marking the descent towards the harbour at Puerto de la Aldea. Tenerife lies west across the sea. The road continues northeast, following the cliff. There are one or two further spots where cars can pull off the road, sometimes with difficulty, so take care. As the Andén Verde draws to a close the road swings inland, descending towards the little village of El Risco.

Artenara

At 1,219m above sea level and dominated by a statue of Christ, this pleasant little town of distinctive white houses is the highest on the island.

Every window, balcony or turn of the road offers thrilling views – from its northern side towards the pinewoods of Tamadaba (▶ 46), and from its southern side across the wide valley in which the Roque Bentaiga (▶ 43) rises in solid splendour. The surrounding landscape is riddled with caves, some of them in continuous habitation since pre-Spanish times. The biggest attraction here is the small but none-the-less charming, cave church, the Santuario de la Virgen de la Cuevita (the Sanctuary of the Virgin of the Cave). Only 8m across, with a vaulted roof, the 14th-century image of the Virgin and Child stands above an altar and pulpit hewn out of solid rock, possibly by Franciscan monks. A restaurant, La Silla (▶ 64), can be reached through a rocky tunnel bored right through the end of the ridge which the town straddles.

INFORMATION

+ C2
- Municipality of Artenara: 49km southwest of Las Palmas, 91km north of Playa del Inglés
- Good restaurants in town (€–€€€)
- 220 from Las Palmas
- Tamadaba (▶ 46)
- Fiesta of Santa María de la Cuevita, last Sunday in Aug: grand occasion with cycling competition and torchlit processions

Santuario de la Virgen de la Cuevita

Barranco de Guayadeque

INFORMATION

🔲 E3

✉ Municipality of Agüímes:
30km south of Las
Palmas, 28km northeast
of Playa del Inglés

🍴 Several cafés in Barranco;
Tagoror restaurant (€€)

🚌 11 or 21 to Agüímes

♿ None

❓ Access on foot or by car
from Agüímes or Ingenio
(➤ 50)

*In the Barranco de
Guayadeque*

An enchanting canyon southwest of the airport, on the eastern side of the island, and a centre of population in pre-Spanish times.

Lying between the municipalities of Ingenio and Agüímes, this *barranco* is more praised by environmentalists than any other on the island. From the flat floor of the dry river bed the walls of the ravine rise, through green terraces of cultivation, through tall palms, eucalyptus and the soft green ping-pong bats of prickly pear, to lofty crags of red volcanic rock.

Many of the island's rarest plants live here, and much of the *barranco* has been designated a nature reserve. The 80 endemic species of flora found here include the *kunkelliela canariensis* and *helianthemum tholiforme*.

The aboriginal people who once lived in this fertile valley left behind hundreds of caves, natural and man-made, that served as homes, animal shelters and grain stores. The many burial chambers found here form an important part of the Guanche exhibits of the Museo Canario in Las Palmas (➤ 38). The area is little inhabited today, but the 50 or so inhabitants are probably the most direct descendants of this prehistoric aboriginal world. They still farm, keep animals and live in caves. They even park their cars in cave garages. In Roque, the one small hamlet on the valley floor, there are cave homes, restaurants and a cave church. The area's most famous restaurant, however, is the Tagoror (➤ 64), right at the end of the *barranco* in a series of caves overlooking the valley. The stream beds under the trees make a pleasant and popular picnic spot during the weekends.

Caldera de Bandama

The splendid volcanic *caldera* or crater of Bandama forms a perfect bowl, 1km across and 200m deep, with no way out at the bottom.

Its steep but gentle-seeming slopes are made up of dark grey ash, but the floor of the crater is patchily fertile, containing a single farm with chickens and goats, figs, oranges, palms and potatoes. The farmer, Juan, is something of a local celebrity. You can walk down into the crater (it takes about one hour) from the tiny hamlet of Bandama, taking a path past the church. Take care, though, as the steps soon peter out and the track is rough. Bandama, named after a Dutchman, Daniel van Damm, who arrived in 1560 and planted vines here, has a small bar which serves excellent roast pork and red wine.

There are superb views from the immediately adjacent Pico de Bandama *mirador* (574m), the peak itself being a large pimple on the volcanic rim. The *mirador* is popular with coach parties during the day and courting couples at night, with some resulting wear to the crater's upper slopes.

On the seaward side of the crater there are lofty views over the two Tafiras (Alta and Baja) and across to the peninsula of La Isleta and the city of Las Palmas. On the west side of the crater is the Club de Golf Bandama, the oldest golf club in Spain. It was founded in 1891 by the British community who had settled in Santa Brígida and the neighbouring Tafiras. The club moved from Las Palmas up to this marvellous site on the edge of the crater in 1956. The accompanying Hotel Golf Bandama is comfortable but seriously sporty. It's owned by a naturalised Spanish Swede and patronised mostly by Scandinavians, Japanese and the local upper classes.

INFORMATION

- E2
- Municipality of Santa Brígida: 10km south of Las Palmas, 52km north of Playa del Inglés, 2km south of Tafira Alta, reached via GC110 from Las Palmas
- Club de Golf bar (€€), Las Geranios bar in village (€€), opening times erratic
- 311 from Las Palmas

Casa de Colón

INFORMATION

➕ E1
✉ Calle de Colón 1
☎ 928 31 23 73
🕐 Mon–Fri 9–6, Sat–Sun 9–3. Closed public hols
🍴 Near by
🚌 1, 2, 3
🎟 Free
↔ Catedral de Santa Ana (► 29)

Once the governor's residence, this fine building now houses exhibits recalling the age of exploration.

When Juan Rejón founded the city of Las Palmas in 1478, among the first buildings he erected was a residence for the governor of the island. When Christopher Columbus arrived on the island on his first voyage of discovery in 1492, he presented his credentials to the governor and lodged in his house. This house, much restored and refurbished, is now an excellent museum, the Casa Museo de Colón.

The house is built around two courtyards of elegant stone, decorated with Canarian balconies of dense, dark tea pine wood. Twelve rooms on two floors contain the permanent exhibitions; those dealing with the four voyages of Columbus to the New World are the most fascinating. A copy of the log of the first journey is left open at the page referring to the stop for repairs in Las Palmas.

Replica ships in the Casa de Colón

Among the intriguing displays are nautical maps, as fanciful and crude as a child's drawing; navigational instruments, ingenious and inventive but looking hopelessly inadequate to the modern eye; the tiny ships, and the names of the seamen who manned them. All recall the magnitude of the explorers' task and the courage needed to fulfil it.

Other highlights in the museum include a life-sized reconstruction of the poop deck of the explorer's ship *Nina*, copies of Columbus's early charts and instruments, and a copy of the 1494 Treaty of Tordesillas, which effectively divided the undiscovered world between Spain and Portugal. There is also some excellent material on the history of Las Palmas itself and a small collection of 16th- to 19th-century paintings is on show, loaned from the Prado in Madrid.

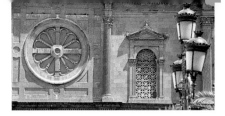

Catedral de Santa Ana

Begun at the end of the 15th century, Las Palmas' cathedral was not finally completed for another 500 years.

A mixture of Gothic, Renaissance, baroque and neo-classical styles reflects the fact that, although this cathedral was begun in 1497, it has only recently been completed and cleared of scaffolding. The west front, designed by local architect Luján Pérez and completed in the early 19th century, faces the large, palm-lined square of Santa Ana and the two groups of bronze dogs which, some feel, gave the island its name (▶ 51). Because of building works the cathedral is reached through the Museo Diocesano de Arte Sacro (Diocesan Museum of Sacred Art). Here there is a fine, if limited, collection of polychrome sculpture; otherwise the religious paintings and liturgical objects on display are generally unremarkable. The museum building and courtyard, however, are beautiful, and a real reward in themselves.

INFORMATION

🔲 E1
✉ Plaza Santa Ana
🚌 1, 2, 3
🔘 Moderate
↔ Casa de Colón (▶ 28)

Diocesan Museum and Cathedral
☎ 928 31 48 89
🕐 Mon–Sat 10–4:30, Sat 10–1:30. Cathedral: daily 10–8; tower: 9:15–6
🔘 Moderate

Palms line the square in front of the Catedral de Santa Ana

Cenobio de Valerón

INFORMATION

✚ C1

✉ Municipality of Santa
María de Guía: 21km west
of Las Palmas, 73km
north of Playa del Inglés

☎ 928 21 94 21

🕐 Mon–Fri 9–2

🍴 None

🚌 103, 105 from Las Palmas

💷 Free, but guard is pleased
with a small gratuity

This network of around 300 cave dwellings is one of the most important archaeological sites of the pre-Hispanic inhabitants of Gran Canaria.

It was once thought that the complex, in a rocky cliff a few miles east of Santa María de Guía, was the home of ancient Guanche priestesses, or *Harimaguadas*, who served the god Alcorac; or that it housed young noblewomen in the period before marriage, when they were fed a calorie-rich diet in preparation for motherhood. Now scholars agree that the caves were used as a forti-fied grain depository, indicating a high degree of social organisation.

The caves, under a red-yellow basalt arch, like the upper jaws of a great fish, appear from a distance like a colony of swallows' nests, made up of round and rectangular chambers. They are reached by a series of winding, steep stairs cut into the rock and interspersed with the occa-sional platform.

Early writers described their astonishment on first seeing the Cenobio de Valerón, the round arch, the intricate complex of caves connected by steps and passages, and the towers (now disappeared) at either side of the entrance, overlooking the *barranco*. Its construction can have been no mean achievement for a people who had no apparent knowledge of metals and used only stones and animal bones for making tools.

Today, concerns for safety and the work of preservation have effectively put much of the complex out of bounds to tourists. It is therefore sadly no longer possible to clamber about inside the caves and explore the site. However, climbing up to this extraordinary place and seeing for yourself the evidence of this Stone Age culture which lasted until well into the 15th century is still a fascinating experience.

Las Palmas

The largest city in the Canary Islands lies like a long (14km) and narrow ribbon on the island's northeast tip, barred from the sea by a highway.

There are four distinct zones of interest: Vegueta, Triana, Ciudad Jardín and Playa de las Canteras. Vegueta (➤ 48), the monumental historic centre, adjoins Triana, a commercial district with fine examples of *modernista* architecture, a style of flowing curves and curious shapes similar to art nouveau. Ciudad Jardín (Garden City) is a leafy suburb created by British merchants in the 19th century, where you will find the Parque Doramas; and a quick hop across town takes you to Parque Santa Catalina and the splendid beach, Playa de las Canteras (➤ 40).

Growth of the city was slow until 1883, when the modern port was begun. Now it is a major international shipping terminal, handling oil and other traffic between Europe and South America.

INFORMATION

➕ E1
✉ 52km north of Playa del Inglés
ℹ Tourist information office in the Parque Santa Catalina
☎ 928 26 46 23
🍴 Many, throughout city (€–€€€)

On the beach in Las Palmas

Maspalomas

INFORMATION

✚ D4

✉ Municipality of San
Bartolomé de Tirajana:
58km southwest of Las
Palmas, 6km southwest of
Playa del Inglés

🍴 Cafés everywhere
(€–€€€)

🚌 Frequent service from
Playa del Inglés including
1, 30; 30 from Las Palmas

↔ Playa del Inglés (➤ 41),
Dunas de Maspalomas
(➤ 31)

Maspalomas still has an up market image, no doubt due to its magnificent dunes and the early building of luxury hotels around the oasis.

The lighthouse (*faro*) and the bus and taxi terminus mark the western boundary of the resort. From here a promenade runs past chic shopping centres, bars and restaurants and ends at the Barranco de Maspalomas, which, at this seaward point, is occupied by a fenced-off lagoon (*charco*) with reed beds, pampas grass and resident and migratory birds. Environmentalists are making themselves heard in the debate between developers and conservationists, particularly in relation to the dunes and the lagoon, and there is a useful Information and Interpretation Centre behind the Hotel Riu Palace in Playa del Inglés. Beach and dunes stretch eastwards from here to join the sands at Playa del Inglés.

North of the lagoon the *barranco* turns into a dry river course with the prestigious 18-hole Maspalomas Campo de Golf to one side. Estates of small, select apartments soon give way to denser holiday accommodation, skirted

Apartments in the resort town of Maspalomas

by wide avenues bearing the names of tour operators like Tui, Thomson and Neckermann. The Faro 2 *centro comercial* is a circular complex of shops, bars and restaurants. Amusement parks mark the resort's northern edge.

Mundo Aborigen

Here you can explore the world of the Guanchos, the aboriginal population of Gran Canaria wiped out by the settling Spanish in the 15th century.

This open-air museum recreates a Stone Age settlement spread across the upper hillsides of the Barranco de Fataga. Life-sized figures of early Guanches occupy caves and stone-built houses, milling flour, cooking, performing a trepanning operation or participating in a religious ceremony. Their social hierarchy, their system of agriculture and knowledge of medicine – herbs, surgery, mummification – are clearly demonstrated and explained in Spanish, English and German.

Mundo Aborigen is based on the chronicles of the first invaders, who found the aboriginal people living in well-organised, close-knit communities. They are invariably described as gentle and kindly, lovers of sport and music and redoubtable in battle.

The spirit of the Guanches is most strongly evoked in the beauty of the hillside and the views from this spot. To the west, dark striated gorges recede into the distance, and to the south, at the mouth of the *barranco*, lies the white city of Playa del Inglés and the Maspalomas dunes.

INFORMATION

- ✚ D4
- ✉ Carretera de Fataga
- ☎ 928 17 22 95
- 🕐 Daily 9–6
- 🍴 Café and souvenir shop on premises (€€)
- 🚌 18 from Maspalomas
- 💰 Moderate
- 🔁 Arteara (➤ 50)

Reconstruction of the Guanche life in the Mundo Aborigen

Museo Canario

INFORMATION

- E1
- Calle Dr Verneau 2
- 928 33 68 00
- Mon–Fri 10–8, Sat–Sun 10–2. Closed public hols
- Good cafés near by (€–€€€)
- 1, 2, 3
- Inexpensive

This excellent museum, dedicated to the prehistory of Gran Canaria, offers a glimpse into the lives of the neolithic inhabitants of the island.

The *Guanches*, as the first inhabitants of the Canary Islands are known, were of proto-Berber, Cro-Magnon and Mediterranean stock, many of them tall and fair-haired. Exhibits show that they lived in caves, as well as stone houses. They kept livestock and grew cereal; they ground grain with millstones and used pestles and mortars. They mummified their dead in the same way as the ancient Egyptians and you can see the long gallery of skulls, skeletons and mummies wrapped in cloth of *junco* (reeds) and goatskin. They were experts in leather and cane work and made fine pottery, although seemingly without the benefit of the wheel. Although they had no written language they left many examples of rock engravings depicting humans, animals and geometric symbols. The famous Painted Cave of Gáldar (Cueva Pintada), unfortunately closed to the public during conservation work, is reproduced in this museum.

The islanders were ruled by kings, or *guanartemes*, practised sports such as wrestling and cross-stick fighting (still popular among modern Canarios), and, according to contemporary accounts, they loved music and dancing. The first Europeans described the inhabitants as generous, simple and trusting. However, when it became clear that their visitors, armed with superior weapons (the Guanches had no knowledge of metal and had never seen a horse), were intent on invading and enslaving them, they resisted them with courage and skill. Indeed they kept up this resistance for most of the 15th century, but were finally defeated by their Spanish conquerors in April 1483 at Forteleza Grande.

Palmitos Parque

Spread over 200,000sq m at the head of the Barranco de Chamoriscán, this park is one of the island's principal attractions.

Exotic birds flourish here – 1500 different species, many of them uncaged – including flamingoes, toucans, cranes, macaws, hornbills, peacocks and tiny hummingbirds.

Winding paths lead from one point of interest to another, past a stream, a palm grove (there are 51 varieties among 1,000 palms) and clumps of giant euphorbia, to a small island, home to a couple of white gibbons. The heated butterfly house has butterflies from all over the world, and the orchid house, said to be the first in Spain, is also spectacular. There are plenty of shady benches and cafés.

The park was first opened in the 1970s and has been regularly extended and improved since then. A 1,000sq m aquarium in a dramatic natural setting, with vast concave glass tanks set in rock surrounds, provides a panoramic view of tropical fish from the Pacific region and the Amazon.

A favourite with children is the parrot show. A well-trained troupe of macaws walk tightropes and ride bicycles to the audience's enthusiastic applause. The birds of prey are also popular.

INFORMATION

➕ C4
✉ Barranco de Chamoriscán: 55km southwest of Las Palmas, 15km northwest of Playa del Inglés
☎ 928 14 02 76
🕐 Daily 10–6
🍴 Cafés and souvenir shops in park (€€)
🚌 Free bus services from Playa del Inglés, San Agustín and Puerto Rico
💰 Expensive
🔄 Aqua Sur (► 57)
❓ Parrot and birds of prey shows through the day

Cacti flourish in Palmitos

Playa de las Canteras

INFORMATION

🔵 E1

✉ Las Palmas

☎ Tourist information office
at Parque Santa Catalina,
☎ 928 26 46 23

🍴 Cafés on and behind the
beach (€–€€€)

🚌 1, 2, 3, 20, 21

🛳 Boats to Cádiz on Spanish
mainland, jetfoil to
Tenerife and ferries to all
Canarian islands from
passenger port

♿ None

🔄 Vegueta (➤ 48)

Its position is extraordinary: backed by the hotels, shops and businesses of a major city, Las Canteras beach stretches in a golden curve, its waters warmed and sheltered from the wind by the presence of the inshore reef known as La Barra.

Playa de las Canteras marks the north-western seaward edge of the city of Las Palmas. 2.6km long, a programme of improvements resulted in the planting of palm trees on the sands, and the re-building of a wide and attractive promenade, the Paseo de las Canteras, behind the beach. The huge range of restaurants which line the promenade reflect the different nationalities of seamen who have settled here; Bulgarian, Korean and Japanese, German, British and Swedish can all be found in this cosmopolitan strip.

Before the modern age of mass air travel, visitors to Gran Canaria always arrived at Las Palmas by liner, and tourism had its early beginnings in the north here, right behind Las Canteras beach. Older residents speak of a time when Las Canteras even boasted its own sand dunes, like Maspalomas, before the development of the town.

Summer weekends find the beach almost as crowded as those in the south of the island; its fans comprise foreign visitors and local Canarios who prefer the slightly cooler, occasionally cloudy days of the north, where the prevailing northeast trade winds form clouds as they hit the mountains. There is a good choice of hotel accommodation, pensions and apartments, many of them with sea views. As for restaurants and nightlife, visitors will find all they expect from a beach resort, combined with the usual offerings of a sophisticated modern city; but in the end, the beach itself is the star (➤ 54).

Playa del Inglés

An uncompromisingly new resort town, the first sight of Playa del Inglés, as you swing south on the motorway from the airport, is not reassuring. It has all the marks of haphazard, unplanned and hastily assembled accommodation in a concrete sprawl.

Once inside the resort, the first-time visitor is likely to get lost among identical streets with identical hotels. There is no obvious town centre, no charming plaza with shady trees and outdoor cafés, of the kind that you will find in any true Canarian town. Most of the life, apart from that of beach and hotel, is concentrated in the rather grim commercial centres (*centros comerciales*). These are buildings of several storeys, often with one or two below ground level, containing hundreds of small units of shops, bars, restaurants and entertainments. They are worth visiting only in the evening, when they become animated; and even then, they may become too animated for some tastes.

But the real plus sides of Playa del Inglés are simple, the sunshine is almost guaranteed, the beach is splendid and the resort has plenty of everything most tourists want: accommodation in every category, from the luxury hotel to cheaper pensions, restaurants to suit every palate and purse and representing every national cuisine, with diversions – again, to suit all tastes – for every hour of the day and night.

It is also well-served with buses, taxis and car hire agencies and even a miniature train, so that moving around is a simple matter. A great deal of money has been spent on planting trees and flowers in public areas. In the early evening the heart of Playa del Inglés is the long coastal promenade, the Paseo Costa Canario, which runs along the coast from San Agustín to Maspalomas.

INFORMATION

➕ D4

✉ Municipality of San Bartolomé de Tirajana: 52km south of Las Palmas. Tourist Information Office: Centro Comercial Yumbo

☎ Tourist Office: 928 76 25 91

🍴 Numerous (€–€€€)

🚌 30 from Las Palmas; numerous local buses

↔ Maspalomas (➤ 36)

The bright lights of Playa del Inglés

41

Puerto de Mogán

INFORMATION

* B4
* Municipality of Mogán: 81km southwest of Las Palmas, 29km northwest of Playa del Inglés
* Many cafés and restaurants in resort (€–€€€)
* 1 from Las Palmas, 32 from Playa del Inglés
* Lineas Salmon boat to Puerto Rico, Arguineguín

Often referred to as Little Venice, Puerto de Mogán is a low-rise resort in the southwest of the island, complete with an attractive marina.

Until the 1980s this was simply a fishing village at the mouth of the Barranco de Mogán, providing shelter for a community of hippies and bohemians as well as for local residents. The hippies moved out – most unwillingly – as the first concrete mixers arrived to create a new tourist *urbanización*. Mutterings of rebellion against the continuing *massification* of the coast were silenced here, however, as apartments with prettily painted door and window surrounds, pedestrianised streets, canals and bridges and, above all, hibiscus hedges and roof gardens tumbling with bougainvillea, began to appear in the new Puerto de Mogán. Now, the resort is seen as an example of a tourist building style which does not violate the natural landscape.

Puerto de Mogán has a curved, grey, sandy beach protected by a breakwater, with sun beds and a beach restaurant. The project was designed, however, for boating enthusiasts rather than beach lovers: the marina remains the main focus. If you continue strolling to the very end of the harbour, the views out to sea from the terrace of the El Faro bar/restaurant make it a pleasure to linger over a drink. Diversions include a trip in the Yellow Submarine, a genuine submersible (free bus service from major resorts). You can gaze at the splendours of the deep for 40 minutes out of your very own porthole. For the more active, the choice extends from diving (day or night), or learning to dive, to sailing (mono-hull or catamaran, with or without a skipper) and deep sea sport fishing for marlin, tuna or barracuda. Shark fishing is also popular .

Roque Bentaiga

This dramatic monolith, raised like a rugged forearm with clenched fist, surges up to 1,404m from its own rocky massif, set in a broad valley.

Visible from many points in the west and centre of the island, it is accessible by (a very wiggly) road. For the aboriginal inhabitants of the island it was a sacred place and a scene of sacrifices. Bentaiga also made a most effective fortress, playing an important role in the resistance against the Spaniards. Its defenders, under cover of darkness, finally retreated from here to Ansite, where they congregated for their last stand. About 2km along the road from the Bentaiga/El Espinillo turning, in the westward extension of the massif, is the Cueva del Rey, a large, man-made cave, once painted, with side-chambers and floor holes.

INFORMATION

➕ C2

✉ Municipality of Tejeda: 46km southwest of Las Palmas, 35km north of Playa del Inglés

🔁 Roque Nublo (➤ 44)

❓ Half an hour's climb from the parking area on track signed to Bentaiga

The distinctive outline of Roque Bentaiga at sunset

Roque Nublo

INFORMATION

➕ C2

✉ Municipality of Tejeda:
48km southwest of Las
Palmas, 37km north of
Playa del Inglés

↔ Roque Bentaiga (➤ 43)

Though it is a little lower in altitude than the island's highest point at Pico de las Nieves (1,803m compared to 1,949m), this spectacular basalt monolith dominates many views in the centre of Gran Canaria.

It appears to be the final, seemingly irreducible core of a far higher volcanic mountain, formed about 3.5 million years ago, in the island's second great wave of volcanic activity. Its present state is the result of a long process of peeling away by wind, water, snow and ice. There is another, smaller rock, El Fraile ('the priest'), standing close to Roque Nublo. For a closer view of these spectacular formations and some breathtaking views of the rest of the island, there is a footpath from the car park to the rocky plateau from which the Roque Nublo rises, and a footpath right round the little massif (➤ 17).

Roque Nublo rises above the church in Tejeda

Santa María de Guía

Usually known simply as Guía, this town is situated 3km east of its neighbour and friendly rival, Gáldar. Cheese tasting is a must and there is no question of leaving without having taken part!

As in Gáldar (➤ 50), it pays to leave the main road and enter the old quarter, climbing briefly if steeply up narrow but stately streets (start where the road makes an awkward bend). The Las Palmas to Gáldar highway bypasses Guía and has restored the town to its early serenity.

Among the early settlers of Guía were Genoese bankers and merchants, so the town has the benefit of some fine architecture, such as the 16th-century Casa Quintana. As usual, the centrepiece is an old-fashioned main square with trees and a church (Santa María) in stern volcanic grey and white – in this case, however, with a floridly neo-classical façade designed by José Luján Pérez, Canarian sculptor–architect and native son of Guía. Begun in 1607, and mixing baroque with neo-classical, the interior of Santa María is colonial in feeling. The elegant town hall, in Canarian style, is also in the square. Guía is well known for craft, but its most famous product is *queso de flor* ('flower-cheese'), made using goat's milk flavoured with artichoke flowers, best bought at Santiago Giol. This is a great barn of a shop, with cheeses laid out on bamboo mats, old photos of cheeses and cheese-makers, and wine bottles stacked all the way up the walls.

INFORMATION

➕ C1
✉ Municipality of Santa María de Guía: 24km west of Las Palmas, 76km northwest of Playa del Inglés
🍴 Cafés in town (€–€€€)
🚌 103, 105 from Las Palmas
🔄 Cenobio de Valerón (➤ 30)
❓ Santiago Giol, Calle Marqués del Muni 34

The church of Santa María

Tamadaba

INFORMATION

➕ B2

✉ Municipality of Agaete:
57km west of Las Palmas,
99km northwest of Playa
del Inglés

*Tamadaba's pine forest
sweeps down through
the barrancos*

Pinar de Tamadaba, the island's largest forest of Canary pines, is much loved by walkers and picnickers.

Located eight kilometres from the isolated village of Artenara in the northwest of the island, this enchanting green landscape is centred on the Pico de Tamadaba, at 1,444m and scattered with cistus and thyme.

There is a forestry station on the circular road leading round the mountain and an ICONA (national environmental agency) picnic site on the edge of the woods. There are splendid views from the summit down across the surrounding countryside to the coast and, on a clear day, as far as Spain's highest mountain – Mount Teide on Tenerife – 3,718m high and over 60km away.

LA ATALAYA

This once entirely cave-dwelling village 5km west of Santa Brígida continues to produce the kind of hand-made pottery first made by the aboriginal Canarios, without the use of the wheel and unglazed.

➕ E2 ✉ Municipality of Santa Brígida: 12km south of Las Palmas, 52km north of Playa del Inglés 🚌 311 from Las Palmas

MOYA

Seen from the west, Moya is an astonishing place, with a huge church, Nuestra Señora de la Candelaria, perched on the lip of a deep ravine. Small wonder that earlier churches on the same site collapsed into the *barranco*: the first in 1671, the next in 1704.

➕ D1 ✉ Municipality of Moya: 31km west of Las Palmas, 90km north of Playa del Inglés 🍴 Cafés in town (€–€€€) 🚌 127 from Las Palmas

SAN BARTOLOMÉ DE TIRAJANA

A quiet, agricultural town on the lip of the Caldera de Tirajana, wander its steep streets and quiet squares and you will find a world far removed from the parched beaches of the south: a pastoral landscape of orchards and cultivated terraces. It is famous for its local liqueur, *guindilla*, distilled from the sour cherry.

➕ D3 ✉ Municipality of San Bartolomé de Tirajana: 52km southwest of Las Palmas, 24km north of Playa del Inglés 🍴 Cafés (€–€€€) 🚌 18 from Maspalomas; 34 from Agüimes

SAN AGUSTÍN

Southern Gran Canaria's first shovelful of tourist concrete was laid in San Agustín. Curiously, this resort, a step away from Playa del Inglés (➤ 54), has never been tarred with the brush of mass tourism. The resort is cut in two by the 812 highway, leaving the hillside connected to the beachside by bridges. The main beach is the Playa de San Agustín.

➕ D4 ✉ Municipality of San Bartolomé de Tirajana: 48km southwest of Las Palmas, 4km northeast of Playa del Inglés

TELDE

Telde is Gran Canaria's second largest town. Historically, it was the seat of the aboriginal king, or *guanarteme*, who controlled the eastern part of the island. The old town centre is the best bit, while the most picturesque part is the *barrio* of San Francisco – with stone-coigned white houses, wooden balconies and pitched roofs around the 18th-century church.

➕ E2 ✉ Municipality of Telde: 21km south of Las Palmas 🚌 12

TEMISAS

Sometimes known as 'Little Jerusalem', Temisas is a village halfway up a mountainside, famous for its rural architecture – white stone houses with pink-tiled roofs, windows with wooden shutters, a little 18th-century whitewashed church, a water mill and hillsides dotted with olive trees.

➕ D3 ✉ Municipality of Agüimes: 35km south of Las Palmas, 33km north of Playa del Inglés 🍴 Bar in village (€) 🚌 34 from Agüimes

PLACING THE NAME

The name 'Gran Canaria' first appeared on a Spanish map in 1339. The historian Pliny the Elder (AD 23–79) called the island 'Canaria', a possible reference to the large dogs (from the Latin *canis*, 'dog') which he reported living on the island. It is unlikely that the native canary – a small brown finch with a poor singing voice – had anything to do with the matter.

Telde

51

Museums and Buildings

FAMOUS SON

The former home of Juan de
León y Castillo, the engineer
who built the harbour at Las
Palmas in 1882, is now a
museum. The house is located
in the town of Telde (➤ 51).
Casa Museo León y Castillo
✉ Calle León y Castillo
43–45 ☎ 928 69 13 77
🕐 Mon–Fri 9–1 🎟 Free

*At Castillo de la Luz in
Las Palmas*

CENTRO ATLÁNTICO DE ARTE MODERNO (CAAM)

This sparkling white gallery, housed in a grand
mansion, in one of the most picturesque streets of
Las Palmas, shows the work of contemporary artists,
mostly Spanish but some Canarian.

🔲 E1 ✉ Calle de los Balcones 9–11, Las Palmas ☎ 928 31 18 24
🕐 Tue–Sat 10–9, Sun 10–2. Closed Mon 🍴 Cafés near by (€–€€€)
🚌 1, 2, 3 🎟 Free

CUATRO PUERTAS

Cuatro Puertas (Four Doors) was a major religious
site, used for worship and sacrifice by the aboriginal
people of Gran Canaria. There are four cave
openings, leading to a single chamber.

🔲 E2 ✉ Municipality of Telde: 19km south of Las Palmas 🍴 None
on site; bar in village below (€) 🚌 35 from Agüimes or Telde 🎟 Free

LA GUANCHA

On an arid site, hemmed in by houses and banana
plantations, substantial remains of pre-Hispanic
dwelling places and communal tombs survive.

🔲 C1 ✉ Municipality of Gáldar: 29km west of Las Palmas, 81km
northwest of Playa del Inglés 🍴 Bar in El Agujero (€) 🎟 Free

MUSEO ELDER

Excellent museum of science and technology with
over 200 exhibits. You can watch chicks hatch, go
inside an F5 plane and explore sound.

🔲 E1 ✉ Parque Santa Catalina, Las Palmas ☎ 828 01 18 28;
www.museoelder.org 🕐 Tue–Sun 10–8. Closed Mon and some public
hols 🍴 Café in museum (€) 🚌 1, 2, 3 🎟 Moderate (IMAX extra)

MUSEO NÉSTOR

The life work of the island's most famous painter,
Néstor Martín Fernández de la Torre, 1887–1938, is
displayed in this museum in the Pueblo Canario.

🔲 E1 ✉ Pueblo Canario, Las Palmas ☎ 928 24 51 35
🕐 Tue–Sat 10–8, Sun and hols 10:30–2:30. Closed Mon. 🍴 Café
in Pueblo Canario (€) 🚌 1 🎟 Moderate

PUEBLO CANARIO

The Pueblo Canario, the Canarian Village, is an attempt
to preserve, recreate and display the best of Canarian
architecture. There is a pretty courtyard, with outdoor
café tables, restored church and a covered arcade of
small shops selling Canarian handicrafts.

🔲 E1 ✉ Parque Doramas, Las Palmas 🍴 Pueblo Canario Bodegón
(€€) 🚌 1 ❓ Traditional music and dance Sun 11:30AM

Views

Looking into the Caldera de Bandama

EL FARO RESTAURANT

From the balcony of this restaurant right at the end of the harbour at Puerto de Mogán, nothing separates you from the wild, blue Atlantic. Look back over the marina and the dark mountains behind.

➕ B4 ✉ Puerto de Mogán ☎ 928 56 52 85 🕓 Lunch, dinner

MASPALOMAS DUNES

Evening light dancing on a calm sea, the dramatic swoop and fall of shadows as the day ends among the wind-sculpted dunes – a constant delight in Gran Canaria (➤ 16).

➕ D4 ✉ 10-minute walk towards Playa del Inglés from the lighthouse at Maspalomas

MESÓN DE LA SILLA

10-minute walk through a passage bored through rocks on to the terrace of this restaurant giving sudden and breathtaking views of the peaks of Roque Nublo and Roque Bentaiga.

➕ D2 ✉ Artenara, Camino de la Silla 7 ☎ 928 66 81 08
🕓 Lunch only

MIRADOR DEL BALCÓN

This lookout point is one of the highlights of a magnificent corniche drive along the Andén Verde on the north west of the island with views of tumbling cliffs and hillsides covered in *tabaiba* and *carde*.

➕ B2 ✉ 11km from San Nicolás on the GC200

PICO DE BANDAMA

From the lookout point, there is a fine view westwards over the extinct Bandama volcano, shaped like a perfect bowl, with a working farm at its base and a prestigious 18-hole golf course on its rim.

➕ E2 ✉ Pico de Bandama, Municipality of Santa Brígida: 10km south of Las Palmas

PINAR DE TAMADABA

The remains of a high pine forest in the centre of the island with cistus and thyme underfoot. A walk through the pines is delightful; the views from the higher peaks over Agaete and Ténerife are spectacular.

➕ B2 ✉ Follow signs from Artenara to Tamadaba – 8km; forestry station has information on walking routes

ISLAND WALKERS

Walking in the mountains is a popular activity on Gran Canaria, particularly with the younger generation. Older folk remember a time when there were few roads on the island and walking was the only method of transport. Not surprisingly, they prefer to ride in motor cars. *Caminos Reales*, literally 'royal ways', are a network of paths once guaranteed by royal authority. They now form the basis of many of the island's walking tracks.

Beaches

El Oasis Beach at Maspalomas

LAS CANTERAS
The town beach of Las Palmas, capital city of the island, is 3km long. Its wide golden sands are backed by a fine promenade, the Paseo de las Canteras, lively with bars, restaurants and hotels; its waters, protected by a natural reef, La Barra, are always calm and clear.
➕ E1 ✉ C/ Nicolás Estévanez or another parallel street, Las Palmas
🚌 1, 2, 3, 20, 21

MASPALOMAS
A magical beach of wide, golden sands with a lighthouse at the western end, a freshwater lagoon and sand dunes up to 30m high. On the extreme southern tip of the island, the sea-swell can be strong.
➕ D4 ✉ Maspalomas 🚌 30 direct service from Las Palmas; numerous local buses

PLAYA DEL INGLÉS
This 4km-long stretch of sand is what brings most people to the island. Backed by an attractive promenade, the Paseo Costa Canario, and then by less attractive hotel and apartment blocks, the beach at Playa del Inglés joins the dark sands of San Agustín at one end to the golden dunes of Maspalomas at the other.
➕ D4 ✉ Playa del Inglés 🚌 30 from Las Palmas

PUERTO RICO
This gently curving beach is an artificial construction, being built with sand brought in by boat from the Sahara. Calm and safe, it's ideal for families with young children, but can get crowded.
➕ B4 ✉ Puerto Rico, Municipality of Mogán 🚌 1, 91 from Maspalomas; 32 from Playa del Inglés/Maspalomas

SAN AGUSTÍN
At one end of the long beach that joins the resorts of San Agustín to Playa del Inglés and Maspalomas, this 600m beach is backed by an upmarket resort of smart hotels surrounded by spacious gardens.
➕ D4 ✉ San Agustín, Municipality of San Bartolomé de Tirajana

SARDINA
In the municipality of Gáldar, this small, secluded beach, situated beneath dark volcanic cliffs, is quiet and little-visited. Clear waters among the rocks near by attract divers.
➕ B1 ✉ Sardina, near Gáldar 🚌 103, 105 from Las Palmas to Gáldar, then taxi to Sardina

Parks

In the Top 25

PARQUE DORAMAS

This shady park, in the middle of Ciudad Jardín,
contains the Hotel Santa Catalina, the Pueblo
Canario and the Museo Néstor. Doramas, after whom
the park was named, was the last Guanche king of
Eastern Gran Canaria.

✚ E1 **✉** Ciudad Jardin, Las Palmas **◷** Daily **🍴** Cafés (€–€€€)
🚌 1 **♿** Free

PARQUE SANTA CATALINA

The liveliest public space in Las Palmas, this park is
surrounded by pavement cafés. Korean and Russian
seamen mingle with African street-traders and
tourists from northern Europe, while Canarians play
chess and dominoes. Perfumeries and bazaar-like
shops fill up the side streets, which also act as a red
light district by night.

✚ E1 **✉** Santa Catalina **🍴** Many cafés around (€–€€€)
🚌 1, 2, 3 **ℹ** Tourist information office **☎** 928 26 46 23
↔ Playa de las Canteras (➤ 40)

PARQUE SAN TELMO

A shady square full of tall palms and benches, this
park is famous for its kiosk café, overtly decorated in
the *Modernista* style, and for its charming small
church, the Ermita de San Telmo. The church was
rebuilt in the 17th century after destruction by Dutch
pirates. On the west side of the park a stern neo-
classical building guarded by soldiers is the
headquarters of the Spanish army in the Canary
Islands. It was from here, in 1936, that General
Franco announced his opposition to the Republican
government, so beginning an insurrection which
became the Spanish Civil War.

✚ E1 **✉** Corner of Calle Bravo Murillo and Avda Rafael Cabrera
🍴 Many cafés around (€–€€€) **🚌** 1, 11, 41

LOS TILOS

The name refers to the surviving one per cent of
Gran Canaria's original and ancient *laurisilva* (laurel)
forest, still holding on here under rigorous protection.
You may survey it from the very narrow road that runs
through it but you are not allowed to wander in it.
This is a tiny nature reserve, only 200m long, up
almost vertical banks from the stream bed.

✚ D1 **✉** Municipality of Moya: 34km southwest of Las Palmas,
87km north of Playa del Inglés **?** On minor road off 150 Moya-Guía
road, 3km from Moya

*A fragment of laurel
forest remains at
Los Tilos*

55

Children's Activities

CENTRAL GRAN CANARIA AND THE NORTH

Any trip to a cave church or a restaurant in a cave (Artenara ➤ 25) is at least a novelty for young people, but there is not much to entertain children in the north or centre, with the exception of Reptilandia Park in Gáldar (✉ Carretera Norte ☎ 928 55 12 69), where poisonous snakes, alligators, lizards and turtles can be seen in a pleasant hillside park, plus a parrot on a perch that calls out 'Hola. Que tal?' ('Hallo. How are you?'), as you approach.

LAS PALMAS
MUSEO CANARIO

A museum full of mummies, skulls and skeletons is bound to be a hit with many children (➤ 38).

✚ E1 ✉ Calle Dr Verneau 2 ☎ 928 33 68 00 🕐 Mon–Fri 10–8, Sat–Sun 10–2. Closed public hols 🚌 1, 2, 3

MUSEO ELDER

State-of-the-art interactive museum of science and technology. Fun for all the family.

✚ E1 ✉ Parque Santa Catalina s/n 35007 ☎ 828 01 18 28 🕐 Tue–Sun 10–8 (summer 11–9) 🚌 1, 2, 3

PARQUE DE SAN TELMO

There is a children's recreation area in this park, and children might enjoy the tiles and curves of the popular kiosk café.

✚ E1 ✉ Corner of Calle Bravo Murillo and Avda Rafael Cabrera 🚌 1, 11, 41

PARQUE SANTA CATALINA

If you are visiting the city during any of the fiestas, particularly if you are here at Carnival, take the children to the special children's shows here, early each evening. Enjoy music, dancing, laser shows and entertainments on a huge stage.

✚ E1 ✉ Santa Catalina ☎ Tourist Information Office 928 26 46 23 🚌 1, 2, 3

PLAYA DE LAS CANTERAS

A child-friendly beach is an incomparable advantage in a city where few entertainments are provided especially for children.

✚ E1 ✉ Las Palmas ☎ Tourist Information Office at Parque Santa Catalina 928 26 46 23 🚌 1, 2, 3, 20, 21

AGÜIMES
CROCODRILO PARK

The largest collection of crocodiles in Europe, as well as other animals, is housed here. Many rescued from cruelty and neglect, including a family of Bengal tigers.

✚ E3 ✉ Carretera Gral Los Corralillos km 5.5, Villa de Agüimes ☎ 928 78 47 25 🕐 Daily 10–5. Closed Sat 🚌 Buses from southern resorts and Las Palmas; enquire at local tourist office

Aqua Sur near Maspalomas

MASPALOMAS
AQUA SUR

Day-long fun in pools and water slides, at this very popular water park.

✚ D4 ✉ Carretera Palmitos Parque km 3 ☎ 928 14 05 25 🕐 Daily, summer 10–6, winter 10–5 🚌 45, 70 from Maspalomas

CAMELLO SAFARI DUNAS
A camel ride is always popular, and an even bigger treat when the progress is through the famous desert-like sand dunes of Maspalomas. Don't forget to wear sun hats as you are very exposed to the sun. The Fataga and Chamoriscan *barrancos* also have safaris.

➕ D4 ✉ Avda Dunas s/n ☎ 928 76 07 81 🕐 Daily 9–4:30
🚌 Plaza del Faro, 29, 30, 32

HOLIDAY WORLD
Completely rebuilt, this fun park has everything for a great evening out for all the family – roller coasters, roundabouts, arcades and plenty of restaurants.

➕ D4 ✉ Carretera General Las Palmas ☎ 928 73 04 98 🕐 Daily 6PM–midnight 🚌 45, 70 from Maspalomas

PALMITOS PARQUE
Although children love the performing parrots, this is much more than a parrot park. There is a great aquarium and attractive snack bars and cafés.

➕ C4 ✉ Barranco de Chamoriscán ☎ 928 14 02 76 🕐 Daily 10–6 🚌 Free bus from Maspalomas, Playa del Inglés, Puerto Rico

PLAYA DEL INGLÉS
MINI-TREN
This miniature train chunters around a circular route in Playa del Inglés starting from the El Veril commercial centre on Avda Italia.

➕ D4 ❓ Train usually leaves every 30 minutes. The service is run privately and depends on the operator's availability

PUERTO DE MOGÁN
YELLOW SUBMARINE
Journey to the bottom of the sea – well, almost. A submarine trip to see a wreck and marine life.

➕ B4 ✉ Pantalán Dique Sur ☎ 928 56 51 08 🕐 10, 11, 12, 1, 2, 3:30, 4:20, 5:10 🚌 Free bus from resorts

PUERTO RICO
SPIRIT OF THE SEA
Enjoy a 2-hour dolphin search aboard this glass-bottomed catamaran with underwater microphones and cameras. You might even spot a whale! Part of the ticket price goes to research.

➕ B4 ✉ Puerto Rico harbour ☎ 928 56 22 29 🕐 10, 12:30, 3

SAN AGUSTÍN
GRAN KARTING CLUB
This go-kart track – the largest in Spain – even caters for children under five.

➕ D4 ✉ Carretera General del Sur km 46 ☎ 928 15 71 90 🕐 Daily, summer 11–10, winter 10–9

SIOUX CITY
Wild West show with enough jail break-outs, bows and arrows and bullets (fake) for any young person.

➕ D4 ✉ Cañón del Águila ☎ 928 76 25 73 🕐 Tue–Sun 10–5. Closed Mon 🚌 Salcai bus 29

Go-karting at San Agustin

BULL-FRIENDLY FIGHTS
A special tourist-geared bullfight takes place every Thursday in Playa del Inglés, when the bull is not harmed (bullfighting is not as popular on the Canary Islands as it is on the mainland).

Sports and Outdoor Activities

Jet-ski at Puerto Rico

DIVING
AQUANAUTS DIVE CENTER, PUERTO RICO
Run by a Finnish company, which offers daily dives, night dives on Sun and Thu and full-day dives (two tanks) plus introductory courses for learners.
➕ B4 ☎ 928 56 06 55

DIVE ACADEMY, ARGUINEGUÍN
With its own pool for tuition, this PADI Gold Palm centre's first concern is safety.
➕ C4 ✉ Calle Lajilla s/n ☎ 928 73 61 96

DIVE CENTER NAUTICO, SAN AUGUSTÍN
This German-based dive centre has been around since 1972. They offer courses for beginners and take more experienced divers out into deep water.
➕ D4 ✉ IFA Club Atlantic, Calle Los Jazmines 2 ☎ 928 77 81 68; www.tauchschule-nautico.com

FISHING
BARAKUDA 11, PUERTO RICO
Sport and high seas fishing trip, refreshments provided plus tackle and bait. The skipper can provide instruction in English. Book two days ahead.
➕ B4 ☎ 928 73 50 80 🕑 Daily 9ᴀᴍ–1ᴘᴍ

GOLF
SALOBRE GOLF AND RESORT, ARGUINEGUÍN
Fine views towards the sea and mountains. It is an 18-hole, par 71 course with additional driving range, putting green and restaurant.
➕ C4 ✉ Urbanización El Salobre ☎ 928 01 01 03 🚌 32 from Playa del Inglés

CLUB DE GOLF, CALDERA DE BANDAMA
Splendid location on the edge of the Bandama crater, near Santa Brigida: 18 holes, par 71, 5,679m course. Hotel and restaurant attached. Visitors, as temporary members, may play any day except at weekends.
➕ E2 ✉ Carretera de Bandama s/n ☎ 928 35 01 04 🚌 39

CAMPO DE GOLF, MASPALOMAS
Close to dunes and palm groves, this is another splendidly sited golf course: 18 holes, par 73, 6,220m course. Visitors may book lessons, hire clubs and practise on the driving range.
➕ D4 ✉ Avda Neckerman s/n ☎ 928 76 25 81 🚌 30

MOUNTAIN BIKING
HAPPY BIKING, PLAYA DEL INGLÉS
Bikes (one to six days) and rollerblades (by the hour or day) can be hired here. Special weekend rates.
➕ D4 ✉ Hotel Continental, Avda de Italia 2 ☎ 928 76 68 32

RIDING

BANDAMA GOLF CLUB RIDING SCHOOL, BANDAMA
Associated with the golf club, this horse-riding school offers lessons and treks in a dramatic rural landscape.

➕ E2 ✉ Carretera de Bandama s/n ☎ 928 35 20 26

HAPPY HORSE
With an English guide you can go on 1- or 2-hour rides around the Palmitos valley or a 3-hour ride to the beach at Meloneras. All abilities welcome.

➕ C4 ✉ Carretera de Palmitos Parque, Finca 9 ☎ 679 86 70 57

SAILING

PARADISE YACHTING, PUERTO DE MOGÁN
A range of water sports, including sailing, offered here with a choice of monohull or catamaran, with or without a skipper.

➕ B4 ✉ Local 96 ☎ 928 56 55 90

SUPER CAT, PUERTO RICO
Let someone else do the work and relax on one of the biggest sailing catamarans in the world. You can have a swim and partake of the onboard barbecue. Splendid views along the coast. Departs daily at 10.30AM.

➕ B4 ✉ Local 96 ☎ 928 56 55 90

TENNIS

EL TENIS CENTER, MASPALOMAS
There are 11 clay courts and professional help when needed. Squash and a gym, too.

➕ D4 ✉ Avda Tour Operador Tjaereborj, 9 Campo de Golf ☎ 928 76 74 47

WALKING

CANARIAVENTURA, PLAYA DEL INGLÉS
Take a guided walk along the island's paths and get close to nature. You will be provided with water and snacks and even sticks if you need them. Departs Wednesdays at 9AM.

➕ D4 ✉ C C Eurocenter, Planta 2, Local 29 ☎ 928 76 61 68; www.canariaventura.com

WINDSURFING
Most beaches have equipment to hire and offer lessons to beginners and those wishing to improve.

F2 SURFCENTER DUNKERBECK, PLAYA DEL ÁGUILA
Eugen Dunkerbeck runs a school for beginners and provides facilities for those with advanced skills.

✉ Plaza de Hibiscus, Águila Playa ☎ 928 76 29 58

CLUB MISTRAL CANARIAS, PLAYA DE TARAJALILLO
Rents boards all year round and offers lessons to beginners during the summer.

➕ E4 ✉ Playa de Tarajillo ☎ 928 77 40 25

LATEEN SAILING
Lateen sailing is a sport peculiar to this island. Small boats with huge sails race around the Bay of Las Palmas between April and September. Watch them (Saturday afternoon and Sunday morning) from the Avenida Maritima in Las Palmas.

Stables near Palmitos Parque

59

Places to Have Lunch

Food is fun on Gran Canaria

BALCÓN DE ZAMORA, TEROR (€€)
Terrific views while eating good local dishes including kid stew.
➕ D2 ✉ Carretera a Vallesco km 8 ☎ 928 61 80 42

CAFÉ MADRID, LAS PALMAS (€)
Situated in the historic Hotel Madrid. Excellent value menu of the day.
➕ E1 ✉ Plaza de Caivasco 2 ☎ 928 36 06 44

CASA MONTESDEOCA, LAS PALMAS (€€€)
Patio and ground floor of a restored mansion in the old town. Wonderful ambience, great food.
➕ E1 ✉ Montesdeoca 10 ☎ 928 33 34 66

CASA ROMÁNTICA, AGAETE (€€)
Excellent international and Canarian food. Ice cream with fruit from the garden.
➕ B1 ✉ Valle de Agaete, km 3.5 ☎ 928 89 80 84

CHIPI-CHIPI, PLAYA DEL INGLÉS (€€)
Good food, well served, in an unpretentious restaurant.
➕ D4 ✉ Avenida Tirajana, Ed. Barbados 1
☎ 928 76 50 88

LA CANTONERA, VEGA DE SAN MATEO (€€)
Canarian dishes in a museum of Canarian rural life.
➕ D2 ✉ Avenida Tinamar ☎ 928 33 13 74

COFRADÍA DE PESCADORES, ARGUINEGUÍN (€€)
A fishermen's co-operative with an island-wide reputation. Freshest of fish and seafood.
➕ C4 ✉ Avenida del Muelle ☎ 928 15 09 63

EL FARO, PUERTO DE MOGÁN (€€)
Lovely location in the small lighthouse at the end of the fishing harbour. Excellent fish dishes.
➕ B4 ✉ Puerto de Mogán ☎ 928 56 52 85

HIPÓCRATES, LAS PALMAS (€€)
Vegetarian restaurant in the old town. Good service, pleasant atmosphere.
➕ E1 ✉ Calle Colón 4, Vegueta ☎ 928 54 82 51

MARIETA BUFFET GRILL, PLAYA DEL INGLÉS (€–€€)
Popular self-service restaurant with a huge selection and you can eat all you want. Good value.
➕ D4 ✉ Avda Italia, 15 ☎ 928 76 71 661

GRAN CANARIA
where to...

In Las Palmas

PRICES

Prices are approximate, based on a three-course meal for one, without drinks and service:

€   = up to €12
€€ = €12–€24
€€€ = over €24

LAS PALMAS

CAFÉ MADRID (€)

In one of the loveliest squares in the city, this is a good place for a drink or the excellent value menu of the day.

✉ Plaza de Cairasco 2
☎ 928 36 06 64
🕐 Lunch, dinner

CAFÉ VEGUETA (€)

This cafe-bar in the old town offers a snack lunch after sightseeing or a pre-dinner cocktail.

✉ C/Mendizábal 24
☎ 928 33 13 21
🕐 Lunch, dinner

CANGURO (€)

For the biggest croissants and cakes around try this snack bar. A good place for breakfast before looking around Vegueta market.

✉ C/Calvo Sotelo 1
☎ No phone
🕐 Normal shopping hours

CASA CARMELO (€€€)

Excellent grilled meat and fish of your choice. Friendly atmosphere.

✉ Paseo de las Canteras 2
☎ 928 46 89 27
🕐 Lunch, dinner

CASA MONTESDEOCA (€€€)

An elegant dining room and patio restaurant set in a 16th-century restored town house.

✉ C/ Montesdeoca 10
☎ 928 33 34 66
🕐 Lunch, dinner. Closed Sun

EL ACUEDUCTO (€€–€€€)

Intimate restaurant with wooden beams and an open grill. The place for carnovores, with an array of meats grilled to your liking.

✉ Sargento Llagas 45
☎ 928 26 42 42
🕐 Lunch, dinner

DON QUIJOTE (€€)

The flavour here is international, specifically Belgian, with the emphasis on steak.

✉ C/Secretario Artiles
☎ 928 27 27 86
🕐 Lunch, dinner

EL CERDO QUE RIE (€)

Moderate prices for good food, especially flambés and fondues.

✉ Paseo de las Canteras 31
☎ None   🕐 Lunch, dinner

EL CID (€€–€€€)

Atmospheric restaurant serving authentic Canarian cuisine not far from Playa de Canteras. Local meats and fish a speciality.

✉ Tomás Miller 73
☎ 928 27 81 58
🕐 Lunch, dinner

EL CORTE INGLES (€€)

The popular lunchtime restaurant in this prestigious department store serves excellent food from a varied menu.

✉ Avda Mesa y Lopez 18
☎ 928 22 64 49
🕐 Lunch. Closed Sun and hols

EL HORREÑO (€–€€)

A pleasant rustic feel to this excellent restaurant whose owner comes from El Hierro, one of the Canary Islands. The menu reflects traditional Canarian cooking; try the delicious roast pork.

of tourists that this restaurant includes pizzas on its menu. Well-known for its typically Canarian dishes this eatery serves mainly fish plus a good selection of grilled meats.

✉ Bahía Feliz, San Augustin
☎ 928 15 71 79
🕒 Lunch, dinner

MARIETA BUFFET GRILL (€–€€)

One of the many self-service restaurants – good value, huge selections – you really can eat all you want. They do a good hearty breakfast, too, to set you up for the day.

✉ Avda Italia 15, Playa del Inglés ☎ 928 76 71 66
🕒 Lunch, dinner

TERRAZA OASIS (€–€€)

Nice terrace overlooking the sea where you can eat traditional Canarian food at reasonable prices.

✉ Boulevard Faro, Maspalomas ☎ 928 14 51 12
🕒 Lunch, dinner

MOGÁN

GRILL ACAYMO (€€)

Rustic décor combined with thrilling terrace views. Canarian food a speciality.

✉ El Tostador 14
☎ 928 56 92 63
🕒 Lunch, dinner. Closed Mon

PUERTO DE LAS NIEVES

CAPITA (€€)

Freshest fish, excellent service, in this bustling, cheerful restaurant.

✉ Puerto de las Nieves 37
☎ 928 55 41 42
🕒 Lunch, dinner

EL DEDO DE DIOS (€€€)

Seafood soup and fish stew with *gofio* is the speciality here – Canarian fish cooking at its best.

✉ Puerto de las Nieves
☎ 928 89 80 00
🕒 Lunch, dinner

EL PUERTO DE LAGUETE (€€)

Crowded at weekends and never empty during the week, this fish restaurant is famous for its food and its atmosphere.

✉ Nuestra Señora de las Nieves 9 ☎ 928 55 40 01
🕒 Lunch, dinner. Closed Mon

FANEQUE (€€)

This smart restaurant in the hotel Puerto de las Nieves offers high quality, international and Canarian cooking, using both meat and fish.

✉ Avda Alcvade José de Armas
☎ 928 88 62 56
🕒 Lunch, dinner. Closed Sun

LAS NASAS (€€€)

A superb fish restaurant in an area renowned for fish restaurants. Terrace to the beach.

✉ C/Puerto de las Nieves
☎ 928 55 41 94
🕒 Lunch, dinner

PUERTO DE MOGÁN

EL FARO (€€)

A great location in a small 'lighthouse' at the end of the harbour. Sip a drink or attack a grilled fish.

✉ Puerto de Mogán ☎ 928 56 52 85 🕒 Lunch, dinner

LA BODEGUILLA JUANANÁ (€€)

Restaurant combined with a fine delicatessan serving

FISH

Even on an island, demand for fish (*pescado*) can often outstrip supply. Beware of thawed frozen fish sold as fresh. Good, fresh fish is expensive, even if it is bought straight out of the fisherman's nets. Tuna, cod, hake, swordfish, mackerel and sardines are familiar to everyone and are available on most menus. Try the local varieties like *cherne* (similar to bass), *sama* (like sea bream) and, a speciality in Gran Canaria, *vieja* (like parrotfish).

Around the Island

and selling a wide range of local food and handicrafts.
✉ Puerto de Mogán ☎ 928 56 50 44 🕐 Dinner only

CANARIAN BEER

Most Canarios drink beer, *cerveza*, with their food. A small glass of beer is a *caña*. *Tropical* is the major island brand, but *Dorada* from Tenerife is also popular. All international brands are available on the island.

LA COFRADÍDIA DE PESCADORES (€€)

Popular with locals and tourists, this fishermen's cooperative by the harbour produces good fresh grilled fish. Try the warm bread with garlic mayonnaise.
✉ Dársena Exterior del Puerto ☎ 928 56 53 21 🕐 Lunch, dinner

PATIO CANARIO II (€€–€€€)

Specialising in fish, this attractive restaurant also serves grills and Canarian fare.
✉ Puerto de Mogán ☎ 928 56 54 56 🕐 Lunch, dinner

SEEMUSCHELL (€€–€€€)

Seafood specialities from around the world all beautifully cooked and presented in this intimate, pretty little restaurant decked out in pale blue.
✉ Puerto de Mogán ☎ 928 56 54 86 🕐 Dinner only

TU CASA (€€)

Fish is the speciality here. Try the *parrillada de pescado* – variety of grilled fish.
✉ Avda de las Artes 18 ☎ 928 56 50 78 🕐 Lunch, dinner

PUERTO RICO

DON QUIJOTE (€€)

International cuisine at low prices. Children's menu.
✉ Centro Comercial ☎ 928 56 09 01 🕐 Lunch, dinner. Closed Sun

EL TIBURÓN (€€)

Translated as 'the shark', this restaurant offers different types of fresh fish as well as some excellent pizzas. You may be lured in with offers of free *sangria*.
✉ Paseo Marítimo ☎ 928 56 05 57 🕐 Lunch, dinner

GRAN CANARIA (€€)

Not just barbecued meat and fish by the beach here. This restaurant has huge steaks, great desserts – complete with flaming sparklers – and live music.
✉ Playa de Puerto Rico ☎ 928 56 13 54 🕐 Lunch, dinner

LA CANTINA (€€–€€€)

Best know for its wines you can also get a good steak or fondue here.
✉ Apartmentos El Greco, Calle Doreste y Mjolina ☎ 928 56 00 40 🕐 Lunch, dinner

SANTA BRÍGIDA

BENTAYGA (€€)

First-class restaurant which uses the best of fresh, local produce in local cuisine. The meat dishes, particularly lamb and goat, are highly recommended.
✉ Carretera del Centro 130, Monte Coello ☎ 928 35 02 45 🕐 Lunch, dinner

CASA MARTEL (€€€)

Old-fashioned country restaurant which is equipped with an

excellent wine cellar.

✉ Carretera del Centro, km 18, El Madroñal   ☎ 928 64 24 83
🕐 Lunch, dinner

GRUTAS DE ARTILES (€€€)

This establishment enjoys a well-deserved reputation for serving good Spanish food in a lively setting which includes a garden, tennis courts, swimming pool and caves.

✉ Las Meleguiñas, Santa Brígida   ☎ 928 64 05 75
🕐 Lunch, dinner

LOS GERANIOS (€)

Famous for roast and grilled pork and local red wine, this simple village bar is crowded at weekends, so it pays to get here early.

✉ Barrio de Bandama
☎ None   🕐 Lunch, dinner

PIZZERÍA CALIFORNIA (€€)

Tasty pizzas, light meals and sandwiches in a cheerful neighbourhood café.

✉ C/Manuel Hernández Muñoz 5   ☎ 928 64 27 03
🕐 Lunch, dinner

SATAUTEY (€€)

This restaurant of the Hotel Santa Brígida (a working hotel and a hotel training school) wins many enthusiastic plaudits for the quality of its food and service – a convincing testimony to the professionalism of the catering students who are in charge of it.

✉ Real de Coello 2, Santa Brígida   ☎ 828 01 04 00
🕐 Lunch, dinner. Closed Tue–Wed

SANTA LUCIA DE TIRAJANA

HAO (€€)

Good country food is served at wooden tables and benches in this welcoming mountainside village establishment. The restaurant is particularly popular with visitors to the neighbouring Museum of Canarian Life.

✉ C/Tomas Arroyo Cardosa
☎ 928 79 80 07   🕐 Lunch

SARDINA

FRAGATA (€€€)

A fish restaurant that looks like the inside of a frigate, right at the end of the harbour with lovely open views of the sea. Choose your own fish, lobster or crab.

✉ Muelle Nuovo, Puerto de Sardina   ☎ 928 88 32 96
🕐 Lunch, dinner. Closed Mon

LA CUEVA (€€)

A small cave restaurant serving fresh fish, either in the cave or on the terrace outside.

✉ Playa de Sardina   ☎ 928 88 02 36   🕐 Lunch, dinner

MIGUELÍN (€€)

A simple fish restaurant. Each dish is freshly prepared and cooked to order. Excellent value.

✉ Carretera de Sardina, km 5, 79   ☎ 928 88 00 15
🕐 Lunch, dinner. Closed Mon

TAFIRA

JARDÍN CANARIO (€€€)

A wonderful setting on the cliffs above Tafira's botanical gardens. The

VEGETARIANS

Vegetarians may feel sadly neglected in island restaurants despite the quality and variety of local vegetables. A meal consisting only of vegetables is a novel concept to most Canarian cooks, who will happily produce a vegetable stew full of beans, carrots, sweet potatoes and artichokes, then add a blood sausage or pork chop for supposed extra nutrition. Similarly, when you order a salad, it is worth mentioning if you do not want tuna (*atun*) or egg (*huevo*) added.

Around The Island

NIGHTLIFE IN LAS PALMAS
(➤ 79)

There is something in this city for every taste, however mainstream or bizarre. The general rule is: the nearer you are to the Parque Santa Catalina and the later at night, the nearer you are to topless bars, sex shows and to nightlife of a generally louche nature. That is not to suggest, however, that there are no wild night-time entertainments in the Old Town or that you will not find a quiet place to sip a mineral water in a Santa Catalina bar. The venues for young nightlife change with every season. The signs are that the trendiest clubs are in the Las Arenas *centro comercial* and around the marina at Las Palmas. If you turn up at a bar or disco before 10PM, you will find yourself alone.

food is excellent and of Canarian style, the service is elegant.

✉ Carretera del Centro, km 7.200, Tafira Alta ☎ 928 35 16 45 🕐 Lunch, dinner

LA MASIA DE CANARIAS (€€€)

This excellent country restaurant serves wholesome, fresh Canarian food.

✉ C/ Murillo 36, Tafira Alta
☎ 928 35 01 20
🕐 Lunch, dinner

TEJEDA

CUEVA DE LA TEA (€€)

A unpretentious restaurant specialising in roast meat.

✉ C/Dr Hernández Guerra
☎ 928 66 61 28 🕐 Lunch

EL REFUGIO (€€)

Incomparable situation among the high peaks. Offers a Spanish and international menu.

✉ Cruz de Tejeda
☎ 928 66 61 88 🕐 Lunch

YOLANDA (€€–€€€)

Wonderful views from the balcony (across to Tenerife weather permitting). Excellent roast meats served with local vegetables, and some international dishes.

✉ Cruz de Tejeda ☎ 928 66 62 76 🕐 Daily 9–7

TELDE

EL PUNTON (€€)

On the beach at Playa de Melenara, this is an excellent place for lunch, with the 'fish of the day' very good value. Paella ia also a speciality. Popular with the locals.

✉ Centro de Ocio Melenara
☎ 928 13 12 84 🕐 Lunch

LA PARDILLA (€€)

Northeast of Telde, this restaurant is highly praised for its traditional Canarian cuisine, particularly its mojo sauces to accompany charcoal-grilled meat. The *puchero canario* – a rich meat and vegetable stew – is another favourite.

✉ C/Raimundo Lulio 54, La Pardilla ☎ 928 69 51 02
🕐 Lunch, dinner. Closed Mon

TEROR

BALCÓN DE LA ZAMORA (€€)

Fine views from the look-out point and excellent kid stew in this busy roadside restaurant.

✉ Carretera a Vallesco km 8
☎ 928 61 80 42
🕐 Lunch, dinner

VEGA DE SAN MATEO

LA CANTONERA (€€)

Good country cooking in an old farmhouse which has been turned into a museum of rural life and an excellent hotel in lovely surroundings.

✉ Avda Tinamar s/n
☎ 928 33 13 74
🕐 Lunch, dinner. Closed Sun

LA VAGUETILLA (€€€)

This is an ideal restaurant in which to enjoy a long, slow Sunday lunch. Canarian and Spanish food, beautifully cooked and served. Eat in the restaurant or garden.

✉ Carretera del Centro km 20.300 ☎ 928 66 07 64
🕐 Lunch, dinner. Closed Tue

Books, Fashions and Luxuries

BOOKS

LAS PALMAS

LA LIBRERÍA
The best bookshop in Las
Palmas is run by the island
government and stocks a
wide range, including
books on flora and fauna
and guide books.
⊠ C/Cano 24
☎ 928 38 15 39

ELECTRONIC GOODS

LAS PALMAS

MAYA
A reputable chain of
retailers dealing in
cameras, videos, TVs,
mobile phones etc.
⊠ Calle Mayor de Triana 107
☎ 928 37 12 55

VISANTA
Prices are fixed at this
well-established shop and
goods are guaranteed.
There is another branch
on C/29 de Abril and in
the Yumbo Centrum,
Playa del Inglés.
⊠ C/Ripoche 25
☎ 928 27 17 14

FASHION

LAS PALMAS

BLAS
A good choice for jeans,
particularly well-known
brands such as Levis.
⊠ C/Tomás Miller, 67 and
C/Ripoche 21

BOUTIQUE GEMA
Modern clothes for young
women.
⊠ C/Travieso 13
☎ 928 36 27 79

GUCCI
Smart Canarios favour
Italian fashion.
⊠ C/ Viera y Clavijo 6
☎ 928 36 09 80

ZARA
High fashion geared to
young tastes.
⊠ Calle Mayor de Triana 39
☎ 928 38 27 32

PERFUMES

LAS PALMAS

DEFA
Offers a good selection of
cosmetics and perfumes.
⊠ C/Mayor de Triana 21
☎ 928 26 82 18

MAYA
This Maya store sells a
good range of perfume
and cosmetics.
⊠ C/Mayor de Triana 105
☎ 928 37 20 49

YVES ROCHER
A huge range of perfumes
and beauty goods at very
reasonable prices.
⊠ C/Nestor de la Torre 36
☎ 928 24 73 89

TOBACCO

LAS PALMAS

MARQUEZ
Cigars and cigarettes of all
lengths and thicknesses,
including those from the
island of La Palma, said to
be the best in the Canaries.
⊠ C/Ripoche 1
☎ 928 26 56 35

MIGUEL SANTANA
A speciality cigar shop
with a wide range.
⊠ C/Carmen Quintana 20
☎ 928 25 61 04

SHOPPING IN LAS PALMAS

The best places to shop in Las
Palmas are the streets around
the Parque Santa Catalina and
in the Triana district,
particularly the pedestrianised
Calle Mayor de Triana and the
small streets off it.

Food and Drink

OPENING HOURS

Shops open from 10 to 1:30 or 2, and from 4:30 to 8. When they are shut, they are very shut: that is, boarded up, so even window shopping is impossible. The department store El Corte Ingles on Avenida Mesa y Lopez in Las Palmas is open all day. It holds enough stock to satisfy the most compulsive consumer, until everything else opens again after lunch.

LAS PALMAS

CANGURO

Mainly a café, but selling some of the biggest croissants and cakes around.

✉ C/Calvo Sotelo 1

CUMBRES CANARÍAS

This deli stocks sausages and cheeses produced from all parts of the island. Other branches throughout the city.

✉ Tomás Miller 47–49
☎ 928 47 22 46

MORALES

A traditional Las Palmas café selling delicious cakes and pastries.

✉ C/Viera y Clavijo 4; also at Reyes Catolicos 12

ARUCAS

DESTILERÍAS AREHUCAS

The place to buy Arucas' famed rum. You can see barrels signed by King Juan Carlos and Tom Jones and then have a free tasting of both rum and liqueurs. Some of the rums have been aged for up to 12 years. If it is rum-based liqueurs you prefer take your pick from banana, orange, coffee, almond or honey.

✉ Lugar Era de San Pedro 2
☎ 928 62 49 00

MOYA

DORADOS

A fine selection of mouth-watering biscuits and cakes, including the traditional *mimos* and *suspiros*.

✉ C/General Franco 19

SAN BARTOLOMÉ DE TIRAJANA

BAR MARTIN

Guindilla, a locally produced liqueur made from sour cherries, is on sale at this bar.

✉ C/Reyes Catolicos

BODEGA VINO TINTO

Attractive shop with local produce – honey, jam etc and a leaning towards Canarian wines.

✉ C/Reyes Catolicos

SANTA MARÍA DE GUÍA

LOS QUESOS

A veritable cheese emporium with assorted produce of sheep's and goat's milk as well as honey, local wine, rum and craftwork.

✉ Carretera General Lomo de Guillén 17

SANTIAGO GIL ROMERO

The best buy here is the *queso de flor de Guía*, a creamy cheese flavoured with artichoke flowers. Cheese in this fascinating relic of a shop is left to mature on bamboo mats. Seeing is believing at this old-fashioned shop.

✉ C/Marqués de Muni 34
☎ 928 88 18 75

TEJEDA

DULCERÍA NUBLO

Delicious almond sweets and cakes are the speciality here. It is well known for its *mazapan* (almond cake).

✉ C/Dr Hernández Guerra
☎ 928 66 60 30

Handicrafts

LAS PALMAS

ATARECOS
The stock here includes Latin American as well as Canarian handicraft and clothes. Good range of T-shirts. The owner speaks excellent English.
✉ C/Cano 30
☎ 928 43 32 45

FEDAC
The Fundación para la Etnografía y el Desarollo de la Artesania Canaria (FEDAC) is a non-profit public trust for the development of Canarian handicraft and has two outlets on the island. This branch sells decoratively carved bone-handled knives, pottery, traditional musical instruments and basketwork. Sometimes you will find a woman spinning wool by the door to create a suitably artisan ambience. This is the place to contact if you are interested in Canarian crafts from all the islands and to be sure of authenticity.
✉ C/Domingo J Navarro 7
☎ 928 36 96 61

GARA ARTE-SANA
Canarian products of high quality including leather, wood and ceramics. Great for gifts to bring home.
✉ C/Mayor de Triana 51
☎ 928 36 81 48

ORBIS
Sr Miguel Santana Cruz specialises in *timples*, a type of small four- or five-string guitar (► 75) Canarian guitar. Buy off the peg, or you can get one custom-made.

✉ C/Mayor de Triana 51
☎ 928 36 81 48

PUERTA DEL SOL
The speciality of this shop is embroidered shawls in all colours and designs.
✉ C/Secretario Artiles 65
☎ 928 26 94 87

AGÜIMES

ART AGUI
Located in the charming old quarters of Agüimes, this shop sells all types of handicrafts from the Canary Islands, along with books, art and culinary specialities.
✉ Plaza del Rosario
☎ 619 66 62 63

ARUCAS

ADELINA VIERRO
Beautiful examples of Canarian crochet work.
✉ C/Hermanos Carvajal
☎ 928 62 60 29

FELUCO
Small sculptures and objects made of the striking grey basalt stone, *piedra azul*, dug from the local quarries. Picture frames, flowers, a model of the church of San Juan Bautista are all sold here.
✉ C/Dr Fleming
☎ 928 60 54 45

ROBERTO RAMIREZ
The place for walking sticks that are not just functional but carved, sculpted, inlaid, bound and decorated until they become collectors' items; and for extravagantly fanciful kites.
✉ C/ Garcia Guerra 2
☎ 928 60 51 73

ADDED VALUE?

It is no longer true that the Canary Islands are a duty-free haven for bargain-hunters. Admittedly there is no value added tax and there are some minor concessions based on Spain's terms of entry into the European Union. However, these factors do not automatically guarantee low prices. Check out the supermarkets for good prices.

73

Handicrafts

RESORT SHOPPING

Shopping can be a bizarre experience in the southern resorts because, with the exception of Puerto de Mogán, the activity is concentrated in the giant shopping/restaurant/entertainment malls called *centros comerciales*, rather than in shops on streets. These shopping centres are often huge concrete blocks three to four storeys high, connected by stairs and passages. The shops themselves, with one or two exceptions, appear rather tatty and generally stock a limited range of cheap goods.

GÁLDAR

JOSÉ MARRERO

Cuchillos Canarios (Canarian knives), remain an essential tool for every Canarian farmer, but are sold here as collectors' pieces, due to their decorated handles.

✉ C/Clavel 8
☎ 928 88 05 55

LUIS SUÁREZ

Fine basketwork, created in many different shapes and sizes, made from cane and palm leaves.

✉ Apartado de Correos
☎ 928 89 51 82

L'ATALAYA

L'ATALAYA CENTRO LOCERO

This village has long been a centre of pottery production. There is a strong sense of preserving traditional techniques and the ALUD (Association of Professionals of La Loza of La Atalaya) has a programme of continued research and teaching as well as organising the exhibition and sale of items of pottery. Through their work they are passing knowledge on to a new generation.

✉ Camino de la Picota 11
☎ 928 28 82 70

PLAYA DEL INGLÉS

ARTEGRAN

All manner of Canarian handcrafted items on sale here. Products include work in clay, wool, linen and iron. Good place to buy gifts to bring home.

✉ Boulevard El Faro 33, Paseo del Faro, Maspalomas
☎ No phone

LA GALERÍA

A shop in the great warren of the Yumbo Centro carrying a range of island handicraft, as well as items from further afield. There are occasional gems to be discovered here.

✉ Yumbo Centro
☎ No phone

FEDAC

Canarian handicrafts sold at the Tourist Information Office. Fedac's aim is to maintain and develop traditional crafts. The items on sale are guaranteed to be genuine Cnarian craftsmanship and not foreign replicas.

✉ Centro Insular de Turismo, Avda de España (on corner with Avda de los Estados Unidos)

PUERTO DE MOGÁN

CANDLE PALACE

Candles made on the premises come in all manner of shapes, sizes and colour.

✉ Boulevard El Faro 33, Paseo del Faro, Maspalomas ☎ No phone

LA BODEGUILLA JUANANÁ

A craft shop-cum-restaurant selling the best – that is, the most authentic – Canarian produce, be it ceramic bowls or local cheeses, well displayed. Open 12–4 and 7–midnight, unless the owner has gone fishing, when he leaves a notice on the window to that effect. During

Handicrafts and Department Stores

summer months, open evenings only. Closed Mondays. The restaurant serves a menu of nouvelle Canarian cuisine, a far cry from the usual hearty stews.

✉ Puerto de Mogán, local 390
☎ 928 56 50 44

RINCON CANARIO
This stylishly decorated shop stocks a wide range of traditional Canarian handicrafts.

✉ Puerto de Mogán, local 105
☎ 928 56 40 44

SANTA MARÍA DE GUÍA

FRANCISCO TORRES
An excellent place if you are looking for the traditional, decorated Canarian knives to take home.

✉ C/18 de Julio 48
☎ 928 88 16 09

TALLER DE ARTESANIA GUIARTE
Juan Jose Caballero works in wood, making traditional country tools and objects – bowls, spoons, boxes, chairs and stools. He also stocks antiques and virtually anything else, in fact, as long as it is fashioned from wood.

✉ C/Lepanto 9
☎ 928 88 27 79

TALFIRA

LA CALZADA
Located on the right-hand side of the road leading to the Jardín Botánico Canario at Tafira Baja, this artisan shop sells a variety of goods, made in Gran

Canaria, suitable for souvenirs.

✉ Tafira Baja
☎ No phone

TEROR

ARTEGRAN
An opportunity to buy some genuine Canarian products made from simple and pure materials including clay, wool, linen and iron. There are two branches in the town.

✉ C/Plaza de Sintes s/n
☎ 928 61 35 90
✉ C/Huerta 10
☎ 928 63 05 94

VEGA DE SAN MATEO

CARMELO TEXEIRA
A wide range of locally produced wicker basketwork items.

✉ C/Los Chorros 67
☎ 928 66 06 52

DEPARTMENT STORES

LAS PALMAS

EL CORTE INGLÉS
The only large department store on the island is found on both sides of the street. You can buy anything here from local cheeses to perfumes, furniture, clothes and books. Ten-minute bus ride from old town.

✉ Avda Mesa y Lopez 18
☎ 928 26 30 00

MARKS & SPENCER
Familiar clothing and other items in this British chain store.

✉ Avda Mesa y Lopez 34
☎ 928 26 35 83

CANARIAN MUSIC

The *timple* is a small four- or five-stringed Canarian guitar and the *chacara* is the Canarian castanet – both are handcrafted on the island. Since the revival of folk music on the island in the 1970s, traditional music and dance have acquired a special importance. You will find the music of Gran Canaria's most popular folk group, Los Gofiones, in any music shop.

SHOPPING MALLS

If it is shopping centres you want try Las Arenas at the west end of Las Canteras beach in Las Palmas. On three levels, with parking below, it caters for a wide range of tastes, from fashion to traditional gifts, from books to jewellery. There are plenty of restaurants plus sea views. El Muelle in the port area has many well-known fashion outlets including Benetton, Zara and Timberland. It also has restaurants, bars, a cinema with 11 screens and discos on the top level. The biggest centre is at La Ballena, 3km out of Las Palmas on the road to Teror, complete with hypermarket and more than 100 shops.

Needlework, Embroidery and *Centros Comerciales*

NEEDLEWORK & EMBROIDERY

INGENIO

CLÉOFE RAMIREZ

Cléofe creates traditional embroideries in the form of household items such as tray cloths, tablecloths and table mats.

✉ Augustin Ramirez Diaz 3
☎ 928 78 08 60

MUSEO DE PIEDRAS Y ARTESANIA CANARIA

A wide selection of native souvenirs and gifts including needlework and embroidery from Gran Canaria and the rest of the archipelago as well as locally produced basketwork, pottery, herbs and cigars. An interesting range of products made from natural plants featuring the aloe vera plant is used in cosmetics and other local plants are used to make perfume.

✉ Camino Real de Gando 1
☎ 928 78 11 24

POTTERY

INGENIO

TALLER ALMAGRE

Look here for the distinctive traditional Canarian pottery – hand-turned and unglazed.

✉ La Capellania 18
☎ 928 78 27 47

MOGÁN

MIGUEL HERNANDEZ

Traditionally designed pottery 10km inland from Puerto de Mogán.

✉ El Horno 8
☎ 928 15 90 72

CENTROS COMERCIALES

MASPALOMAS

FARO 2

Regarded as the most up-market shopping centre in the whole San Agustín/Playa del Inglés/Maspalomas complex. One of three centres in Maspalomas, the others being Oasis and Veradero, the latter featuring stores such as Chanel, Diesel and Lacoste.

✉ Campo Internacional s/n

PLAYA DEL INGLÉS

YUMBO CENTRUM

This is the biggest commercial centre in the resort. Other centres are Aguila Roja; Alohe; Anexo 11; Cita; El Veril; Gran Chaparral; Kasbah; La Sandia; Metro, Plaza de Maspalomas and Tropical. You'll find almost anything that you could want here.

✉ Avda de los Estados Unidos de Norteamérica 54

SAN AGUSTÍN

SAN AGUSTÍN

The larger of the two commercial centres in town; the smaller one is called El Pulpo.

✉ C/ de las Dalias

SAN FERNANDO

SAN FERNANDO

Along with several other centres, including Botánico, the Mercado Municipal, Nilo and Eurocenter, this is an economical place to shop.

✉ Avda de Tejeda

CERAMICS

Most of the ceramics sold on the island are made in the traditional manner and to traditional designs. These are generally simple objects of everyday use like bowls, plates or jugs. Occasionally you will find copies of pre-Hispanic artefacts, such as the terracotta Mother Earth-type idol figure (the Ídolo de Tara), clay pipes (*cachimbas*), or seals in geometric patterns (*pintaderas*), now fashioned into brooches or pins.

Markets

MARKETS

Always providing a fascinating insight into local culture, the markets of Gran Canaria are excellent places to find locally produced crafts, foods and other produce at authentic local prices. Most Canarian markets open from 7AM until 2PM.

LAS PALMAS

MERCADO DE VEGUETA

The oldest general market in the city, where you can find abundant fish, meat, fruit and vegetables – the variety of potatoes is astonishing. The market is surrounded by small lively bars and *churrerías*.
✉ C/Mendizábal

MERCADO DE LAS FLORES

Arts, crafts and flower market held on Sundays.
✉ Plaza de Santo Domingo

MERCADO DEL PUERTO

Recently renovated market, popular with sailors from ships docked in port.
✉ C/Albareda

ARGUINEGUÍN

FISH MARKET

Held every morning. There is also a general market on Tuesday.
✉ Arguineguín harbour

ARUCAS

SATURDAY MARKET

A busy weekly market, held, as in all major towns, in addition to the permanent municipal market.
✉ Plaza de la Constitución

PUERTO DE MOGÁN

FISH MARKET

As well as another daily fish market where you will find all the local catches, Puerto de Mogán has a general market on Friday.
✉ Puerto de Mogán harbour

SAN FERNANDO

WEDNESDAY AND SATURDAY MARKETS

A general market, two days a week, with a wide range of local goods.
✉ Avda Alejandro del Castillo

TEROR

SUNDAY MARKET

A fascinating selection of local produce, including marzipan cakes from the nearby convent, and the town's very own sausage, *chorizo rojo*. Fortnightly.
✉ Plaza del Pino

VECINDARIO

WEDNESDAY MARKET

A wide variety of products are sold on the weekly stalls.
✉ Avda de Canarias

VEGA DE SAN MATEO

SUNDAY MARKET

Situated at the centre of a richly agricultural community, this market is sufficiently well-respected to attract customers from all over the island.
✉ Avda del Mercado

BARGAIN BUYS

Nobody will be surprised if you bargain over the prices quoted for goods on sale in the *centros comerciales*. You can take the opportunity to haggle over items such as perfumes, leather goods, bags and coats, T-shirts, towels, tablecloths, baseball caps and clothes and electronic products.

CRAFT MARKET

In the Plaza de Maspalomas, Playa del Inglés, an evening craft market is held every day except Sunday. It is open from 6PM–11PM and is a great place for presents.

Film, Theatres, Concerts and Folk Dancing

MUSIC, BALLET, OPERA AND THEATRE

An International Music Festival is held every year in Las Palmas, in January and early February. March and April see the Festival of Opera and, in July, the International Festival of Ballet and Dance is celebrated, including performances of Spanish light opera called *zarzuelas*.

FILM

The International Film Festival of Las Palmas de Gran Canaria has been running since 1999 and is held in March in the Alfredo Kraus Auditorium (► below) – for exact dates contact the tourist office – and has as many as 14 countries competing for a range of awards for 'best of,' for example directors, short films or photography.

MULTICINES LA BALLENA

Based in the shopping and entertainment complex by the southern exit out of town. Mostly foreign and dubbed mainstream films.
- ✉ La Ballena Centro Comercial
- ☎ 928 42 03 35

MULTICINES ROYAL

Another cinema offering a choice of screens and mainstream films.
- ✉ C/León y Castillo 40
- ☎ 928 36 09 54

WARNER

Located in the El Muelle shopping centre near the port, this is a good venue to see the latest releases.
- ✉ Elle Muelle de Santa Catalina, s/n ⏰ See press for details

THEATRE & CONCERTS

AUDITORIO ALFREDO KRAUS

A major venue for classical music concerts and a conference centre right on the beach with sea views.
- ✉ Paseo de las Canteras s/n
- ☎ 928 49 17 70
- ⏰ Ticket office: 10–2, 4:30–8:30

CICCA

The Centro de Inciativas de la Caja de Canarias offers theatre, film, modern dance and ballet, concerts and international music stars.
- ✉ Paseo de las Canteras s/n
- ☎ 928 49 17 70
- ⏰ Ticket office: Mon–Fri 10–2, 4:30–8:30, Sat 10–2

TEATRO CUYÁS

This theatre opened in 2002 in a former cinema in Triana and hosts a range of productions from drama and comedy to ballet.
- ✉ C/Viera y Clavijo s/n
- ☎ 928 36 15 09 🚍 1

TEATRO PÉREZ GALDÓS

This theatre is home to the island's symphony orchestra and operatic society. Closed for restoration at time of writing, but the building is well worth a look. Due to re-open 2004/5.
- ✉ C/Lentini 1 ☎ 928 36 15 09 🚍 1

FOLK DANCING

PUEBLO CANARIO

Many cultures have contributed to the folk dancing styles of Gran Canaria, not least Spanish, Portuguese and Latin American. You can see it accompanied by music played on traditional instruments, twice weekly in the Canarian Village. The folk costumes tend to differ from village to village but are all splendidly colourful.
- ✉ Parque Doramas
- ⏰ Performances Sun 11.30AM
- 🚍 30

Nightlife

LAS PALMAS

CAMEL BAR
Calle León y Castillo is a
popular area for club
venues and not far from
the old part of the city.
You can take a meal and
then dance away the
calories in style.
✉ C/León y Castillo 389
☎ 928 27 23 06 🕒
Mon–Tue 8:300PM–2:30AM,
Wed–Sat 10:30PM–3:30AM

CASINO DE LAS
PALMAS
The smartest place on the
island to risk your fortune,
or watch someone else
risk theirs on craps, black
jack, chemin de fer,
baccarat or roulette.
Formal dress is obligatory
and you should take your
passport as proof of
identity.
✉ Santa Catalina Hotel, Parque
Doramas ☎ 928 23 39 08
🕒 Sun–Thu 8PM–4AM, Fri–Sat
8PM–5AM

CUASQUÍAS
Smart and lively venue for
all age groups to see and
hear top performers. Good
jazz and Latin American
music.
✉ C/San Pedro 2, near Triana
☎ 928 37 00 46
🕒 From 10:30PM–late

EL COTO
As you would expect of a
discotheque in the Hotel
Melia, the ambience is
elegant and the
atmosphere refined – even
on a Saturday night. The
music is usually
international/Latin
American.
✉ C/Gomera 6, Las Palmas
☎ 928 26 76 00

FLORIDITA
Restaurant/bar in the
Triana district. Locals love
the Cuban ambience.
✉ C/ San Nicolas Remedios
10–12 ☎ 928 43 17 40

ICE BAR
As the name implies this
is a cool place for over 21s
to hang out. All chrome
and sleek fittings.
✉ C/Franchy y Roca 18 ☎
928 47 24 54 🕒 11PM–5AM

LA ROMANA
Adjoining the Club
Natación Metropole this
place swings until late.
✉ C/León y Castillo
☎ 928 36 18 03
🕒 11:30PM–5AM

PACHA
Smart disco with a giant
video screen. Live music
on the terrace.
✉ C/Simón Bolívar 3, Las
Palmas ☎ 928 27 16 84

PLAYA DEL INGLÉS

The Centro Comercial
Metro has a solid
following among the
young at Pachá, Joy,
Terraza El Metro. The
Centro Comercial Yumbo
attracts a gay crowd to bars
and discos like Gay Male,
King's Club and Come
Back.

SAN AGUSTÍN

CASINO TAMARINDOS
PALACE
You have to be over 18,
look respectable and carry
identification to gamble
here.
✉ Hotel Tamarindos, C/Las
Retamas 3, San Agustín
☎ 928 76 27 24

DISCO LIFE

Discos, pubs and nightlife in
general are concentrated in
the *centre comerciales* – the
commercial centres, of which
there are many in the
southern resorts. German and
British entertainers often
perform in bars and pubs to
their own national clientele.
Centro Comercial Kasbah,
Playa del Inglés, is the most
popular for dancing or
listening to music: try Meliá,
Roger's, Beckham Bar or
China White Costa.

Las Palmas

PRICES

Prices are for a twin room, excluding breakfast and service tax:

€   = up to €60
€€   = €60–€120
€€€ = over €120

The rates vary enormously, depending on the season and the state of the local economy.

GETTING AROUND

You can stay in Las Palmas and still enjoy a visit to the southern resorts or the centre and north by taking one of the buses run by Global Salcai Utinsa ☎ 902 38 11 10. The bus terminal is at Parque San Telmo, Las Palmas, information ☎ 928 36 83 35. Always double-check bus numbers before making a journey. If you intend to travel a lot by bus on the island the Tarejeta Insular card might be worth considering. It gives a 30 per cent discount. For further details contact the bus station in Las Palmas.

ASTORIA (€€)

A modern hotel near Playa de las Canteras with terrace, swimming pool, gym and squash courts.
✉ C/Fernándo Guanarteme 54
☎ 928 22 27 50

ATLANTA (€€)

Good facilities in this friendly hotel, only a few minutes from the beach. There are 64 rooms and 7 suites, all with air conditioning.
✉ C/Alfredo L Jones 37
☎ 928 26 50 62

CANTUR (€€)

Comfortable, 1960s-built hotel with terrace; many rooms with view of Playa de las Canteras. Breakfast included. 124 rooms.
✉ C/Sagasta 26
☎ 928 27 30 00

COLÓN PLAYA (€€)

An apartment block situated at the beach end of this busy street. Go for the sea-view rooms. 38 rooms.
✉ C/Alfredo Jones 45
☎ 928 26 59 54

CONCORDE (€€€)

A modern hotel with 124 rooms, comfortable and well-run, close to Canteras beach and Parque Santa Catalina. Swimming pool.
✉ Tomás Miller 85
☎ 928 26 27 50

FATAGA (€€)

A middle-range hotel in the business area of the city within easy walking distance of both Canteras and Alcaravaneras beaches. 92 rooms.
✉ C/Nestor de la Torre 21
☎ 928 29 06 14

FAYCAN (€)

A moderately priced, clean and comfortable hotel with 61 rooms in an advantageously central situation.
✉ C/Nicolas Estevanez 61
☎ 928 27 06 50

HOTEL IDAFE (€)

Basic but clean, this hotel with 34 rooms is centrally located, not far from the beach.
✉ C/Nicolas Estevanez 49
☎ 928 27 49 36

HOTEL IGRAMAR (€€)

Only 50m from the beach, this hotel with 61 rooms is clean and comfortable and also offers access for visitors with disabilities.
✉ C/Columbia 12
☎ 928 22 58 40

HOTEL MADRID (€)

Built in 1910, and long favoured by artists and intellectuals, this family-run hotel is slowly being updated. General Franco stayed in room 3 in 1936.
✉ Plaza de Cairasco 2
☎ 928 36 06 64

HOTEL PARQUE (€€)

Well situated for the old town, just across the road from the Parque San Telmo, this is an excellent middle-range hotel. There is an excellent bus service to the southern resorts from the nearby bus station. 102 rooms.
✉ Muelle de las Palmas
☎ 928 36 80 00

HOTEL PUJOL (€)

A good budget hotel with 48 rooms and easy access to the port and to Canteras Beach.

✉ C/Salvador Cuyas 5
☎ 928 27 44 33

HOTEL TRYP IBERIA (€€)
Very comfortable hotel in a good location right on the promenade with panoramic vies of the sea. Facilities include a beauty centre, swimming pool and 297 rooms all with shower.
✉ Avda Alcalde José Ramírez Bethencourt 8   ☎ 928 36 13 44

IMPERIAL PLAYA (€€€)
Pleasant, comfortable hotel on the north end of Canteras beach, complete with satellite TV and air-conditioning. Excellent breakfast. Sauna and squash courts. 142 rooms.
✉ C/Ferreras 1
☎ 928 46 48 54

MAJÓRICA (€)
Right on Parque Santa Catalina and therefore likely to be noisy, this hotel is nevertheless clean and cheap.
✉ C/Ripoche 22
☎ 928 26 28 78

MARSIN PLAYA (€€)
Comfortable apartments facing the beach at Las Canteras. It is worth paying out a little extra to get the sea views.
✉ Luis Morote 54
☎ 928 27 08 08

MELIÁ LAS PALMAS (€€€)
Luxury hotel in the middle of Playa de las Canteras, with 312 rooms, shops, disco and a swimming pool.
✉ C/Gomera 6s
☎ 928 26 76 00

PENSÍON PRINCESA (€)
Basic accommodation only a couple of minutes from the beach. One of the cheapest places to stay in the city.
✉ C/Princesa Guayarmina 2
☎ 928 46 77 04

REINA ISABEL (€€€)
Luxury hotel in an unrivalled position on the Canteras Beach, with a superb high-rise restaurant, Parrilla Reina Isabel, and a gym and swimming pool on the roof terrace. 231 rooms.
✉ C/Alfredo L Jones 40, Las Palmas   ☎ 928 26 01 00

SANSOFÉ PALACE (€€€)
An excellent modern hotel which occupies a fine position near Canteras Beach. 115 rooms.
✉ C/Portugal 68
☎ 928 22 40 62

SANTA CATALINA (€€€)
Gran Canaria's top city hotel, with 208 rooms, in a quiet, shady park. Canarian architecture, fine restaurant and a casino.
✉ León y Castillo 227, Parque Doramas   ☎ 928 24 30 40

TENESOYA (€€–€€€)
This is more a business than a tourist hotel. The facilities are good and the service friendly and efficient. 43 rooms.
✉ C/Sagasta 98
☎ 928 46 96 08

VEROL (€–€€)
Good value hotel with 25 rooms, located just one minute from the beach.
✉ C/Sagosta 25
☎ 928 26 21 04

CAPITAL HOTELS
Although early tourists preferred the north of the island and made their base in Las Palmas, the choice of hotel accommodation in the capital is now rather limited in comparison with what is on offer in the southern resorts. In general, visitors who choose to stay in Las Palmas tend to be business travellers or those in flight from other tourists.

LA GUAGUA TURISTICA
The Las Palmas tourist bus is a great way to see the city. This open-top bus service operates daily from 9:30AM until 5:45PM. Tickets are valid for the whole day and are very reasonably priced. You can get on and off at any stop throughout the day. Commentary is in English, Spanish and German. Tickets are available from the bus station at Parque San Telmo and on the bus itself. The two-hour circuit of the city begins and ends at Parque Santa Catalina.

Around Gran Canaria

AGAETE

HOTEL PRINCESA GUAYARMINA (€€)
An old-fashioned spa hotel in a fertile valley. Ideal for walks in the countryside.
✉ Los Berrazales, Valle de Agaete ☎ 928 89 80 09

LAS LONGUERAS (€€–€€€)
In a beautiful situation, this 19th-century mansion was recently renovated into a country hotel.
✉ C/Doctor Chil 20, Valle de Agaete ☎ 928 89 87 52

AGÜIMES

CASA DE LOS CAMELLOS (€€)
Lovely rural hotel renovated from a 300-year-old stone barn set around courtyards and gardens. Twelve rooms decorated in traditional style.
✉ C/Pragreso 12 ☎ 928 78 78 50

ARGUINEGUÍN

STEIGENBERGER LA CANARIA (€€€)
Luxury hotel. Beautiful gardens, view and pool.
✉ Barranco de la Berga ☎ 928 15 04 00

ARUCAS

LA HACIENDA DEL BUEN SUCESO (€€€)
High quality rural hotel overlooking banana plantations with views to the sea. Pool, jacuzzi and fitness room.
✉ Carretera de Arucas a Bañaderos. km 1 ☎ 928 62 29 45

FATAGA

MOLINO DE FATAGA (€€)
A small, rural hotel in an old *Gofio* mill in the Fataga valley, with offers of camel rides and hearty Canarian cooking.
✉ Carretera Fataga a San Bartolome km 1 ☎ 928 17 20 89

MASPALOMAS/ PLAYA DEL INGLÉS/ SAN AGUSTÍN

DUNAMAR (€€€)
An incomparable position on the beach and the views from sea-facing rooms make this hotel special.
✉ Avda de Helsinki 8, Playa del Inglés ☎ 928 77 28 00

GLORIA PALACE (€€)
Large, well-established hotel in San Agustín with a new thalassotherapy (sea-water therapy) centre (☎ 928 77 64 04) adjacent which is open to non-residents.
✉ Las Margaritas ☎ 928 76 83 00

GRAND HOTEL RESIDENCIA (€€€)
This designer hotel, opened in 2000, is fast becoming one of the most exclusive on the island, with attractive rooms in villas set around a pool.
✉ Avda del Oasis 32 ☎ 928 72 31 00

IFA FARO MASPALOMAS (€€€)
Luxury hotel metres away from the lighthouse after which it is named. The

sea views are glorious, the hotel restaurant, Guatiboa (➤ 66), is one of the best on the island.

✉ Plaza del Faro, Maspalomas
☎ 928 14 22 14

H10 PLAYA MELONERAS PALACE (€€€)

Just west of Maspalomas, this luxury hotel with 351 rooms is beautifully set above the beach. Choice of restaurants and bars, plus two swimming pools.

✉ Playa Meloneras, Maspalomas ☎ 928 12 82 82

MELIÁ TAMARINDOS (€€€)

Luxury hotel in a quiet situation with superb gardens; casino and cabaret on premises.

✉ Las Retamas 3, San Agustín
☎ 928 77 40 90

RIU GRAND PALACE MASPALOMAS OASIS (€€€)

Undoubtedly the most luxurious hotel in the south, the Oasis is situated on the beach, beside the dunes and surrounded by palms.

✉ Playa de Maspalomas
☎ 928 14 14 48

RIU PALACE MELONERAS (€€€)

A grand, white-wedding-cake of a hotel, with apartment chalets on lawns around a pool.

✉ Las Meloneras Urbanitión
☎ 928 14 31 82

PUERTO DE MOGÁN

HOTEL TAURITO PRINCESS (€€€)

A splendid hotel, above the beach, just outside Puerto Mogán.

✉ Urbanización Taurito s/n
☎ 928 56 52 50

SANTA BRÍGIDA

HOTEL GOLF DE BANDAMA (€€€)

A small country house/golf hotel on the edge of the Bandama crater, just 15m from the first hole.

✉ Bandama s/n
☎ 928 35 33 54

HOTEL ESCUELA (€€)

In the cool hills of Monte Lentiscal, this hotel is now a training school as well as a fully functioning hotel, with a splendid dining room, gardens and pool.

✉ C/Real de Coello 2, Santa Brígida ☎ 828 01 64 00

SAN NICOLÁS DE TOLENTINO

LOS CASCAJOS (€)

A friendly hotel with 20 rooms, located 5km from the west coast of the island. This can be a good place for a stop over during the drive around the island (➤ 18).

✉ C/Los Cascajos 9
☎ 928 89 11 65

TEJEDA

EL REFUGIO (€€)

A rural hotel with 10 double rooms decorated in a traditional, cosy manner. The hotel is situated in beautiful countryside and can make an ideal base for a walking holiday.

✉ Cruz de Tejeda s/n
☎ 928 66 65 13

GRAN CANARIA
practical matters

WHAT YOU NEED

	Some countries require a passport to remain valid for a minimum period (usually at least six months) beyond the date of entry – contact their consulate or embassy or your travel agent for details.	UK	Germany	USA	Netherlands	Spain
● Required ○ Suggested ▲ Not required						
Passport/National Identity Card		●	●	●	●	▲
Visa (regulations can change – check before booking your journey)		▲	▲	▲	▲	▲
Onward or Return Ticket		▲	▲	●	▲	▲
Health Inoculations		▲	▲	▲	▲	▲
Health Documentation (➤ 90, Health)		●	●	▲	●	▲
Travel Insurance		○	○	○	○	○
Driving Licence (national or international; Spain national only)		●	●	●	●	●
Car Insurance Certificate (if own car)		●	●	●	●	●
Car Registration Document (if own car)		●	●	●	●	●

WHEN TO GO

Gran Canaria

High season

Low season

19°C JAN	19°C FEB	19°C MAR	20°C APR	21°C MAY	21°C JUN	23°C JUL	24°C AUG	24°C SEP	25°C OCT	25°C NOV	19°C DEC

 Very wet   Wet   Cloud   Sun   Sunshine/Showers

TIME DIFFERENCES

GMT 12 noon	Gran Canaria 12 noon	Germany 1PM	USA (NY) 7AM	Netherlands 1PM	Spain 1PM

TOURIST OFFICES

In the UK
Spanish Tourist Office
79 New Cavendish Street
London
W1W 6XB
☎ 0207 486 8077
Fax: 0207 486 8034

In the USA
Tourist Office of Spain
35th Floor 666 Fifth Avenue
New York
NY 10103
☎ 212/265 8822
Fax: 212/265 8864

Tourist Office of Spain
8383 Wilshire Boulevard
Suite 960
Beverly Hills
CA 90211
☎ 323/658 7195
Fax: 323/658 1061

WHEN YOU ARE THERE

ARRIVING

Most visitors arrive on charter flights direct from western Europe. Visitors from North America may have to fly via Madrid. There is a weekly car ferry service from the Spanish mainland (Cádiz) taking 36 hours, operated by Trasmediterránea (☎ 902 45 46 45 on Gran Canaria).

Gando Airport
Kilometres to city centre

22 kilometres

Journey times

 N/A

20 minutes

15 minutes

Puerto de la Luz Ferry Terminal Journey times
Kilometres to city centre

3 kilometres

N/A

10 minutes

5 minutes

MONEY

The euro (€) is the official currency of Spain. Euro banknotes and coins were introduced in January 2002.
Banknotes are in denominations of 5, 10, 20, 50, 100, 200 and 500 euros and coins are in denominations of 1, 2, 5, 10, 20 and 50 cents and 1 and 2 euros.
Euro traveller's cheques are widely accepted, as are major credit cards. Credit and debit cards can also be used for withdrawing euro notes from ATM machines. Banks can be found in most towns in Gran Canaria.
Spain's former currency, the peseta, went out of circulation in early 2002.

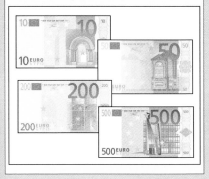

TIME

 Gran Canaria, like the rest of the Canary Islands, follows Greenwich Mean Time (GMT), but from late March, when clocks are put forward one hour, until late September, summer time (GMT+1) operates.

CUSTOMS

 CUSTOMS ALLOWANCES

As the Canaries are a free-trade zone there are no limits on the amounts of alcohol, tobacco, perfume, toilet water and other goods (except for gifts of value greater than 48 Euros) that can be brought into the Islands, but the prices of these products are so low in the Canaries that it seems a pointless exercise to do so. Visitors may bring an unlimited amount of euros or foreign currency in to the Canaries but should declare any amount exceeding the equivalent of 6, 000 Euros to avoid difficulties on leaving.

 NO

Drugs, firearms, ammunition, offensive weapons, obscene material, unlicensed animals.

CONSULATES

UK
928 26 25 08

Germany
928 49 18 80

USA
928 27 12 59

Netherlands
928 36 22 51

TOURIST OFFICES

- Patronato de Turismo
  Gran Canaria (Local Tourist
  Authority)
  León y Castillo 17
  35003 Las Palmas
  de Gran Canaria
  ☎ 928 21 96 00
  Fax: 928 21 96 01
  www.grancanaria.com

- Oficina de Tourimo del Parque
  Santa Catalina
  Parque Santa Catalina
  Las Palmas de Gran Canaria
  ☎ 928 26 46 23

- Centro Insular de Turismo
  (Tourism Insular Centre)
  Avenida de España
  Centro Comercial Yumbo
  Playa del Inglés.
  ☎ 928 77 15 50

- Avenida de Mogán Pueto
  Centro Comercial Puerto Rico
  Puerto Rico
  ☎ 928 56 00 29

- Oficina Municipal de Turismo
  de Agüimes
  Plaza de San Anton 1
  ☎ 928 12 41 83

Most towns and some larger
villages throughout Gran Canaria
have a local tourist office. Times
of opening vary and most close for
the weekend.

NATIONAL HOLIDAYS

J	F	M	A	M	J	J	A	S	O	N	D
2		2	1	3	1			1	1	1	3

1 Jan	New Year's Day
6 Jan	Epiphany
19 Mar	St Joseph's Day
Mar/Apr	Maundy Thu, Good Fri and Easter Mon
1 May	Labour Day
30 May	Canary Island Day
May/Jun	Corpus Christi
15 Aug	Assumption of the Virgin
8 Sep	Birthday of the Virgin Mary
12 Oct	National Day
1 Nov	All Saints' Day
6 Dec	Constitution Day
8 Dec	Feast of the Immaculate Conception
25 Dec	Christmas Day

Most shops, offices and museums close on these days.

OPENING HOURS

○ Shops	● Attractions/Museums
● Offices	● Bars/Restaurants
● Banks	● Pharmacies

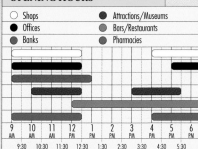

9 AM	10 AM	11 AM	12 PM	1 PM	2 PM	3 PM	4 PM	5 PM	6 PM
9:30	10:30	11:30	12:30	1:30	2:30	3:30	4:30	5:30	

In addition to the times above, some shops in busier resorts stay open
until later in the evening and open on Sunday. Department stores are open
10–8. Some shops (including pharmacies) close Saturday afternoon.
Bank winter opening times are 8–3 (Saturday until 1PM). Banks are
closed Sunday all year. The opening times of museums is variable; some
close Saturday afternoon and all day Sunday, others on Monday (or
another weekday), while some remain open all week.

ELECTRICITY

The power supply is: 220 volts (older
buildings: 110 volts)

Sockets take two-pin
plugs of round-pin
continental style.
Visitors from the UK
require an adaptor and US visitors a
voltage transformer. Power cuts are not
infrequent, so pack a torch.

TIPS/GRATUITIES

Yes ✓	No ✗	
Restaurants (if service not included)	✓	10%
Cafés/bars	✓	loose change
Taxis	✓	10%
Porters	✓	€1–2
Chambermaids	✓	€1–2
Cloakroom attendants	✓	loose change
Hairdressers	✓	10%
Theatre/Cinema Usherettes	✓	loose change
Toilets	✗	

PUBLIC TRANSPORT

Internal-Island Flights
All of the Canary Islands have an airport and are inter-connected by air. The main operators are Avioco (☎ 902 40 05 00) and Air Europa (☎ 928 57 95 84). Flight times are around 30 minutes. Flights between Gran Canaria and Tenerife are almost hourly but early booking is essential.

Buses
Global Salcai Utinsa operate the buses (☎ 902 38 11 10). Services, including express, run from Las Palmas to resorts in the south and to many towns and villages in the centre and the north. Services are reasonably frequent and start from the bus station at Parque San Telmo (☎ 928 36 83 35).
Always check bus numbers and routes used in this guide before making your journey

Internal-Island Ferries
All of the Canary Islands can be reached by ferry, mostly run by Trasmediterránea (☎ 902 45 46 45), departing daily from Puerto de la Luz in Puerto de Las Palmas. There is also a regular jetfoil/hydrofoil service ARMAS (☎ 928 30 06 00) between Las Palmas (Gran Canaria) and Santa Cruz (Tenerife – 100 minutes – and Morro Jable (Fuerteventura). Fred Olsen (☎ 928 49 50 40) runs ferries daily from Puerto de Las Nieves (Agaete) to Santa Cruz.

Urban Transport
In Las Palmas, the numerous Guaguas Municipales (city bus service) runs three routes (1, 2, 3) leaving from the Bus Station Square, the Plaza de Cairasco or General Franco, depending on their destination. City suburb services start from the Plaza del Mercado. Smaller towns such as Telde, Santa Lucía, Arucas, Santa María de Guía and Gáldar, have their own buses.

CAR RENTAL

There are plenty of car-hire firms, usually offering unlimited mileage. Prices vary considerably between large hire companies and small local firms; shop around, keeping in mind that this may reflect genuinely competitive rates or hazardous corner-cutting in maintenance.

TAXIS

Taxis are identified by the letters SP (*servicio público*) on the front and rear bumpers. Most are metered at a rate fixed by the municipal authorities. For short trips in tourist areas the meter will normally be switched off. There are usually fixed rates for long distances.

CONCESSIONS

Students and Youths
For various reasons Gran Canaria and the other Canary Islands do not attract backpacking youngsters the same way as other holiday islands throughout the world. There are only two youth hostels (*albergues*) and only two official campsites on the island. There are few, if any, student or youth concessions available.

Senior Citizens
Gran Canaria is an excellent destination for older travellers, especially in winter when the climate is mild. Some hotels offer long-stay discounts. The best deals are available through tour operators who specialise in holidays for senior citizens.

DRIVING

Speed limits on motorways (*autopista*) and autovias: **120kph**

Speed limits on country roads: **90kph**
Speed limits on urban roads: **50kph**

Speed limits in residential areas: **20kph**

Must be worn in front seats at all times and in rear seats where fitted.

Random breath-testing. Never drive under the influence of alcohol.

Fuel (*gasolina*) is sold as *Super* (4-star), *Normal* (3-star), *Sin plomo* (unleaded) and *Gasoleo* (diesel). Petrol stations are fairly numerous along main roads with 24-hour opening in the larger resorts and towns, though some only open until 2PM on Sunday. In the mountains there are few, if any, filling stations and the steep winding roads cause heavy petrol consumption, so fill up first.

If you break down in your own car the Royal Automobile Club of Gran Canaria, Léon y Castillo 279 (☎ 928 23 07 88), can offer advice on breakdown and repair services. Repairs are usually dealt with promptly. If the car is hired, telephone the local office of the firm and be sure to follow the instructions given in your rental documentation.

PHOTOGRAPHY

What to photograph: wildly varied scenery from the rugged volcanic cliffs and mountain ridges of the western side of the island to the desert-like dunes of Maspalomas in the south.
Restrictions: it is forbidden to take photographs of military bases, military or naval port areas, police, government or military personnel, and inside museums.
Film and camera batteries are readily available and reasonably priced.

PERSONAL SAFETY

Violence against tourists is unusual. Theft from cars is the most common form of crime, particularly in Las Palmas. There are three police forces : Policía Municipal (blue uniforms), Policía Nacional (brown uniforms), and Guardia Civil (pea-green uniforms). To help them and yourselves :

● Do not leave valuables on the beach or poolside.
● Leave valuables in hotel safe deposit boxes.
● Never leave anything of value in your car.
● Avoid the seamier streets of Las Palmas at night.

Police assistance:
☎ **112**
from any call box

TELEPHONES

Light-blue public telephone booths (*Cabina de Teléfono*) are the cheapest to call from. They take coins or a phonecard (*credifone*) available from post offices and some shops. Or use a *telefónica cabin* where the phone is metered and you pay after your call. The code for Gran Canaria is 928.

International Dialling Codes

From Gran Canaria to:

UK:	00 44
Germany:	00 49
USA:	00 1
Netherlands:	00 31

Mainland Spain: dial the full 9-digit number.

POST

Post Offices
Post boxes are yellow. Use the slot marked *extranjero* (foreign) for postcards home. Post offices (*correus*) sell stamps (*sellos* or *timbres*) and provide telegram and fax services. Open: 8:30–8:30 (9:30–2 Sat) Closed: Sun
☎ 902 19 71 97

HEALTH

Insurance
Nationals of EU, and certain other countries, receive free medical treatment in the Canaries with the relevant documentation (Form E111 for UK nationals), although private medical insurance is still advised and essential for all other visitors.

Dental Services
Dental treatment has to be paid for by all visitors. There are many English-speaking dentists; your hotel or tourist information centre will inform you of the nearest one. Private medical insurance will cover dental costs.

Sun Advice
The south of the island experiences virtual year-round sunshine. The sun is at its strongest in the summer months when precautions should be taken. The north of the island is ofter cooler with cloud-cover that provides shade.

Drugs
Prescription and non-prescription drugs and medicines are available from pharmacies (*farmacias*), distinguished by a large green cross. They are able to dispense many drugs which would be available only on prescription in other countries.

Safe Water
Tap water is generally safe but is not recommended for its taste. Anywhere, but especially outside tourist resorts, it is advisable to drink bottled water (*agua mineral*), sold either *sin gaz* (still) or *con gaz* (carbonated).

WHEN YOU ARE THERE

LANGUAGE

Canary Islanders speak Castilian (the language of Mainland Spain). The only difference is in the pronunciation. Islanders don't lisp the letters 'c' or 'z', they are spoken softly. They also speak with a slight lilt, reminiscent of the Caribbean. There are a few indigenous words still in use, the most notable being *guagua* (pronounced wah-wah) meaning bus, and *papa*, meaning potato. In major resorts English is widely spoken but off the beaten track a smattering of Spanish is helpful. Below is a list of some useful words. More extensive coverage can be found in the AA's *Essential Spanish Phrase Book* which lists over 2,000 phrases and 2,000 words.

hotel	*hotel*	breakfast	*desayuno*
room	*habitación*	toilet	*lavabo*
..single/double	*individual/doble*	bath	*baño*
..one/two nights	*una/dos noche(s)*	shower	*ducha*
..per person/per room	*por persona/ por habitación*	en suite	*en su habitación*
		balcony	*balcón*
reservation	*reserva*	key	*llave*
rate	*precio*	chambermaid	*camarera*

bank	*banco*	change money	*cambia dinero*
exchange office	*oficina de cambio*	bank card	*tarjeta del banco*
post office	*correos*	credit card	*tarjeta de crédito*
cashier	*cajero*	giro bank card	*tarjeta de la caja postal*
money	*dinero*	cheque	*cheque*
coin	*moneda*	traveller's cheque	*cheque de viajero*
foreign currency	*moneda extranjera*		

restaurant	*restaurante*	snack	*merienda*
bar	*barra*	starter	*primero plato*
table	*mesa*	dish	*plato*
menu	*carta*	main course	*plato principale*
tourist menu	*menú turístico*	dessert	*postre*
wine list	*carta de vinos*	drink	*beber algo*
lunch	*almuerzon*	waiter	*camarero*
dinner	*cena*	bill	*cuenta*

aeroplane	*avión*	ticket	*billete*
airport	*aeropuerto*	...single/return	*ida/ida y vuelta*
flight	*vuelo*	timetable	*horario*
bus	*guagua*	seat	*asiento*
...station	*estación de guagua*	free	*libre*
...stop	*parada de guagua*	reserved	*reservado*
ferry	*transbordador*	non-smoking	*no fumadores*
port	*puerto*		

yes	*sí*	help!	*ayuda!*
no	*no*	today	*hoy*
please	*por favor*	tomorrow	*mañana*
thank you	*gracias*	yesterday	*ayer*
hello	*hola*	how much?	*cuánto*
goodbye	*adiós*	expensive	*caro*
good night	*buenas noches*	open	*abierto*
excuse me	*perdóneme*	closed	*cerrado*

WHEN DEPARTING

REMEMBER

- Remember to contact the airport on the day prior to leaving to ensure the flight details are unchanged.
- If travelling by ferry you must check in no later than the time specified on the ticket.
- Although there is no restriction on the amounts of alcohol and tobacco you may bring into the Canary Islands, you must comply with the import restrictions of the country you are travelling to (check before departure).

91

Index

TwinPack
Gran Canaria

Written by Gabrielle Macphedran
Designed and produced by AA Publishing
Revision management by Apostrophe S Limited

Published and distributed by AA Publishing, a trading name of Automobile Association Developments Limited, whose registered office is Southwood East, Apollo Rise, Farnborough, Hampshire, GU14 0JW. Registered number 1878835

The contents are believed correct at the time of printing. Nevertheless, the publishers cannot be held responsible for any errors or omissions or for changes in the details given in this guide or for the consequences of any reliance on the information it provides. Assessments of attractions, hotels, restaurants and other sights are based upon the author's personal experience and, therefore, necessarily contain elements of subjective opinion which may not reflect the publishers' opinion or dictate a reader's own experiences on another occasion.

We have tried to ensure accuracy in this guide, but things do change and we would be grateful if readers would advise us of any inaccuracies they may encounter.

First published 2000.
Revised second edition 2002.
Revised third edition 2005

A CIP catalogue record for this book is available from the British Library.

ISBN-10: 0 7495 4338 8
ISBN-13: 978 0 7495 4338 9

Colour separation by Keenes, Andover
Printed and bound by Times Publishing Limited, Malaysia

ACKNOWLEDGEMENTS
All pictures used in this publication are held in the Association's own library (AA PHOTOLIBRARY) and were taken by JA Tims, with the exception of Front Cover (b) windsurfers, (c) woman, (h) beer, bottom boats, Back cover ct (sign), cb (restaurant), taken by Pete Bennett, Front Cover (e) palm tree taken by Des Hannigan, Front Cover (d) sailing dinghy, (g) flower, Back cover b (neon signs), and pages 5a, 6, 12, 13b, 15, 19, 21, 23b, 26a, 26b, 28b, 32a, 32b, 34b, 34c, 35a, 39a, 39b, 40, 41a, 41b, 42, 43a, 43b, 47, 48a, 48b, 50, 51, 54, 55, 59, 61b, 84, 85b which were taken by Clive Sawyer.

A02011
Fold out map © Freytag-Berndt u. Artaria KG, 1231 Vienna-Austria, all rights reserved